D1301172

THE JOSSEY-BASS NONPROFIT & PUBLIC MANAGEMENT SERIES ALSO INCLUDES:

WORKBOOK FOR SEAMLESS GOVERNMENT

Russell M. Linden

WORKBOOK
FOR SEAMLESS
GOVERNMENT

*A Hands-On Guide to Implementing
Organizational Change*

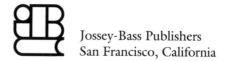

Jossey-Bass Publishers
San Francisco, California

Substantial discounts on bulk quantities of Jossey-Bass books are available to corporations, professional associations, and other organizations. For details and discount information, contact the special sales department at Jossey-Bass Inc., Publishers (415) 433–1740; Fax (800) 605–2665.

For sales outside the United States, please contact your local Simon & Schuster International Office.

Jossey-Bass Web address: http://www.josseybass.com

Manufactured in the United States of America using Lyons Falls Turin Book. This paper is acid-free and 100 percent totally chlorine-free.

Interior design by Claudia Smelser

FIRST EDITION

PB Printing   10 9 8 7 6 5 4 3 2 1

CONTENTS

PREFACE

Since the 1994 publication of *Seamless Government,* I have worked with hundreds of managers who were eager to implement the vision of a seamless or "boundaryless" organization. In such organizations, customers access services in an effortless manner and employees collaborate to achieve desired outcomes rather than fight over turf and resources. In countless workshops and discussions about providing seamless service, people always ask certain questions:

- How do we focus employees on outcomes when we're still measured and held accountable for inputs and outputs?

- How can we move toward seamlessness when those who must lead the change have benefited from the old system and feel they have nothing to gain from change? Interestingly enough, George Washington spoke of the same dilemma in his second inaugural address. Some issues are timeless!

- How do we determine where to start? Which processes are good candidates for redesign?

- How do we align people in our internal units (human resources, finance, accounting, purchasing, and so on) toward this seamless approach when they still believe that their major job is to control—not support—the operational units?

- How can we help our teams get "out of the box" and create dramatically new designs for our work? They've been beaten down in the past when they've tried to be creative or take risks . . . and they have long memories!

- How do we help senior officials remain focused on the change effort? They continually become distracted, and without them, we can't push major change.

- How do we deal with the inevitable resistance?

How, indeed? These are natural, reasonable, appropriate questions, and I was often frustrated when I tried to address them in conversations. The frustration didn't come from a lack of answers; on the contrary, it came from my awareness that there are, in fact, tested and successful approaches for dealing with these questions. Nevertheless, many well-intentioned public servants were flailing around from one trend or fad to another with no apparent awareness of others' successes. This book, then, is an attempt to provide some answers to the ultimate change question—"How?" It's a vital question, it's a straight question, and it deserves straight answers.

That said, I don't pretend that there are simple formulas that will answer each tough "How?" question. Rather, certain themes and approaches are emerging from the success that many agencies are achieving—success that can help all of us. This book pulls together major themes from organizations that are effectively redesigning themselves for seamless service.

WHAT IS THE PURPOSE OF THIS WORKBOOK?

This workbook aims to give practitioners approaches, methods, and tools to help them dramatically improve work processes for seamless service. When these approaches are followed, employees tell me that they fight less over turf and collaborate more to find better ways of serving customers. Walls between units start to collapse, and overall organizational performance improves.

Seamless Government described the concept and principles of seamless service, providing abundant detail and dozens of examples. This workbook doesn't attempt to elaborate on those principles. The word *workbook* is well chosen. Those who use it will find themselves working hard to deliver on this promise.

Understanding how to achieve seamless service doesn't take genius. It requires a method, an awareness of the potential pitfalls, and a good deal of hard work and persistence. I hope this workbook contributes to that noble task.

HOW IS THIS WORKBOOK ORGANIZED?

The workbook is organized by themes, as well as by chapters.

Organization of the Themes: People, Plan, and Politics

The workbook is organized around three *p*'s that together capture the vital aspects of redesigning work. The three *p*'s are *people, plan,* and *politics.*

For any major change to work, leaders must identify and involve certain kinds of *people* to lead projects at different levels. Some roles require great creativity, some need terrific interpersonal skills, and most need great persistence. The key people need to work well together, which means that they must have time to build and nurture relationships.

In addition to people, change leaders need a solid *plan*. It should help them and others anticipate land mines, point people in a common direction, and answer employees' needs for information and guidance but be flexible enough to allow for revisions as conditions change and surprises occur. This workbook provides you with a map for developing your own plan.

But even if an organization has wonderful people and a detailed plan, change is a dicey proposition if the change leaders aren't focused on the *politics* of the situation. I don't mean electoral, partisan politics. No, I am talking about power in organizations. Most significant change efforts can affect the distribution of power; who gets what; and roles, relationships, and resources. This workbook offers numerous tips and approaches for anticipating political needs, responding to political changes and conflicts, and creating a constituency for change that can give your change effort tremendous momentum.

People, plan, and *politics.* These are the three *p*'s that tie the workbook's methods and tools together.

Organization of the Chapters

The workbook is organized into three parts that reflect the three phases of the model I offer. Part One details the initial phase of a change effort—getting ready for change. Chapter One briefly summarizes the concept of seamless service. Chapter Two introduces the model and the key preconditions for change. In Chapter Three, I look at the roles needed when redesigning work processes: a design team, the team's leader, subject matter experts, a project sponsor, a steering team, and a process owner. And Chapter Four is devoted specifically to the steering team's vital work.

Part Two focuses on the steps involved in redesigning work processes. Chapter Five introduces the four key steps for redesigning work. Chapters Six through Nine are then devoted to each of these steps: mapping the current process, establishing desired outcomes, setting stretch objectives, and designing from a clean sheet.

Part Three deals with implementation, which is unfortunately overlooked in most major change efforts. Few change efforts fail because the staff couldn't come up with creative new ways to do the work. Rather, failure, or lack of significant progress, typically comes from inattention to execution. In Chapter Ten, I look at the art of writing a "business case" that summarizes how the process currently works, offers a new design for the process, shows the costs and benefits of that new design, and provides guidance on how to implement it. Chapter Eleven highlights another overlooked aspect of change—communication. There are tips on communications throughout the workbook, but this chapter focuses exclusively on communication methods that are effective and ineffective and communication strategies that involve many people in the change effort. Chapter Twelve details aspects of implementing the approved design: identifying the roles to be played, scheduling the phases and steps, planning and learning from the pilots, phasing in the short-term and longer-term changes, dealing with those who oppose and resist the new design, and so forth.

In the Afterword, I discuss the three most important elements in all major change efforts: courage, heart, and persistence. I don't know how to put courage into a flowchart; heart doesn't lend itself to performance measures; nor can persistence be placed on an organization chart. Yet, as anyone who has experienced the exhilaration of a successful change effort knows, we don't succeed without these precious aspects of human character. I offer some thoughts on how to find and nourish courage, heart, and persistence.

The workbook concludes with six appendixes, which give the reader more specific details on some of the methods described in the chapters. Appendix A details a series of focus groups I conducted for the U.S. Forest Service. It includes the methodology used, the design of each focus group session, the questions asked, and the organization of the final report. Appendix B describes a stakeholder gap analysis, a fairly sophisticated tool for quantifying the needs of different stakeholder groups. Appendix C provides the basic steps for doing a benchmarking study of other organizations. Benchmarking has become very popular in recent years, but many groups jump into their studies with no real understanding of the benchmarking method. This appendix gives the reader some guidelines. Appendix D offers five hands-on exercises for generating creativity. Design teams and others will have fun using these exercises; moreover, they will find that these exercises help to unleash the creative child in each of them, which will help them to come up with wonderful new ideas as they redesign their work. Appendix E shows how to do a value-added analysis of work processes and what to do with the information generated by the analysis. Finally, Appendix F gives guidance on the use of two powerful planning tools: Program Evaluation and Review Technique (PERT) and Critical Path Method (CPM).

WHO SHOULD READ THIS WORKBOOK?

Who should read this workbook? Everyone interested in learning a proven method for making major organizational change.

This workbook is for those who participate in organizational change projects. It is especially useful for organizations that are trying to change their work processes. Many groups of people participate in such projects, and the workbook is designed to help each type of group.

Design Team Members

Those who work on design teams and do the actual redesigning will benefit greatly from reading this workbook. For them, it will

- Serve as a map through the design phase

- Provide instruction about when and how to use certain tools and methods

- Indicate the key people to include and the steps to take

- Clarify the roles of the design team, project sponsor, and other people involved in changing the organization

Design team members should read the whole workbook.

Project Sponsors

Senior managers who agree to sponsor a major change will also benefit from this workbook. Although sponsors do not need the same in-depth knowledge of the steps and tools that design teams will use, they do need to understand their own roles, the roles of design teams and senior steering teams, the likely barriers and points of resistance during the design phase, and the ways in which they can anticipate and negotiate those barriers. By reading the workbook, project sponsors will also learn the critical importance of communication during change projects and the most and least effective communication approaches.

Sponsors should especially focus on Chapters One through Five, as well as Chapters Ten and Eleven.

Senior Organizational Leaders

Organizational leaders, especially those who serve on steering teams that oversee change projects, should read this workbook to learn the basic methodology of redesigning for seamless service. They will gain important knowledge about their roles and those of the project sponsor and design team during the change process. Perhaps most important, senior managers and leaders will learn ways to anticipate the political crises that can undermine change efforts, ways in which they can stay connected to the change effort, and the key roles they will play in approving projects and supporting team leaders.

Organizational leaders should especially focus on Chapters One through Five, Ten, and Twelve.

Those Interested in Leading Major Organizational Change

Individuals who want to help others redesign their work processes should read this workbook. Redesigning work for seamless service is more than employing a methodology or set of tools; it becomes a way of thinking and seeing possibilities. Those who wish to teach and lead others will begin to appreciate this way of thinking if they become familiar with the concepts and methods in this workbook. They should read the entire book.

AND ON A PERSONAL LEVEL: WHY I LOVE TO TALK ABOUT THESE IDEAS WITH MY KIDS

A quick glance through this workbook will reveal a number of flow charts, worksheets, graphics, matrixes, tools, and methods that have helped many teams improve their work processes. It's good stuff if you've been given a large mandate to change something and aren't sure where to start, but what in the world does it have to do with two kids named Becca and Josh who are, at the time of this writing, thirteen and eleven years old?

If we step back to look at the outcomes that seamless service delivers, we will see that it has everything to do with our kids. When employees and their external stakeholders let go of turf, mistrust, bruised egos, feelings of isolation, and a sense of being forgotten and replace them with a close connection to each other and to the work that they share, wonderful things happen. Walls give way to partnership. The insatiable quest for recognition and money gives way to a realization of the meaning in one's work. And the terrible feeling of isolation yields to a growing sense of community.

Partnership, meaning, community. Pick up virtually any newspaper—is there any doubt how much our society needs those precious values? Seamless service can help our organizations deliver those outcomes. And that's why I love talking about it with my children.

February 1998   Russell M. Linden
                                                                Charlottesville, Virginia

ACKNOWLEDGMENTS

This is great fun, naming the people whose ideas, feedback, tough criticisms, and thoughtful additions went into this workbook.

We'll start with John Stephens, a manager in the Public Works Department in Lynchburg, Virginia. John has served as a project sponsor for two re-engineering efforts, and he was truly made for that role! There may be people with a better combination of pragmatism, thoughtfulness, and political and personal sensitivity, but I have yet to meet them. John made especially helpful comments on the first draft of this workbook. He works with a whole crew of wonderful redesigners, people who are working long and hard to make Lynchburg run even better: Paula Gucker, Bill Perkins, Martha Wallace, Woody Wigglesworth, and many others. Their feedback on using the methods in this workbook has informed and broadened my thinking.

Brian Sutton is another class act who made an enormous contribution to this workbook. His sharp mind, incredible grasp of current management thinking, and experience with major organizational change are (as kids say these days) awesome. His unselfish sharing of time and ideas amazed and delighted me.

Prince William County (Virginia) is a very progressive local government with smart, creative people who are helping to write the book on the effective, humane use of performance measures. Martha Marshall is one of their best, and her comments on an earlier draft of this workbook reflect her intuitive feel for teams, models, methods, and the way one integrates those to make a cohesive project. Craig Gerhart, deputy county manager in Prince William County, taught me about the importance of persistence and strong leadership in leading a major change effort.

There are many people who contributed to this effort without knowing it. Gene Rouleau, a wonderful trainer and consultant who worked at the Office of Personnel Management for years before going off on his own, frequently shares with me his experiences in helping agencies redesign their work. Dan Madison, a creative consultant who works to improve processes in private and public sector organizations, has shared many ideas and methods. Jerry Bramstedt, a manager at the Farm Services Administration in the Department of Agriculture, gave me helpful feedback as he and his colleagues used these methods and tools to redesign an important process.

Some people taught me through the force of example about the possibilities and problems of implementing seamless service. They are leaders in the truest sense of the term—people who chart a course, include others in figuring out how to get there, and demonstrate courage in the face of countless roadblocks. That group includes Chuck Short, director of the Montgomery County (Maryland) Department of Health and Human Services; Richard Stevens, county manager of Wake County (North Carolina); Maria Spaulding, director of the Wake County Human Services Department; Donnie Ebanks and Peter Gough (who are leading a huge change in the Cayman Islands government); Chuck Church, Lynchburg (Virginia) city manager, and his colleagues Curtis Randolph and Tyler St. Clair, to name just a few.

My thanks also go to the leaders of several fine educational institutions in which I've had the opportunity to teach and test my ideas with government managers and executives: Curt Smith, Terry Newell, and others at the Federal Executive Institute; Jacqueline Rogers, Susanne Slater, Phil Lee, and Tom Kennedy at the University of Maryland's School of Public Affairs; and Bob Havlick and his colleagues at the Innovation Groups.

Finally, special thanks to Tammie Tyler for tireless help designing graphics, photocopying, editing, making suggestions, and helping me stay focused. Great job!

R.M.L.

THE AUTHOR

Russell M. Linden is a management consultant who specializes in re-engineering and other organizational change methods. Since 1980, he has helped government, nonprofit, and private sector organizations develop leadership, foster innovation, and improve organizational performance. He is an adjunct faculty member at the University of Virginia, at the University of Maryland, and at the Federal Executive Institute. He writes a column on management innovations for the *Virginia Review,* at which he serves as contributing management editor, and he has produced national video conferences on re-engineering and on the human side of change.

Linden has studied innovative organizations in Japan and the United States. He has advised Vice President Al Gore's National Performance Review on reinventing government and on other change methods.

The author of numerous articles, Linden published his first book, *From Vision to Reality: Strategies of Successful Innovators in Government,* in 1990. His most recent book, *Seamless Government: A Practical Guide to Re-Engineering in the Public Sector,* was published in 1994 and was excerpted in the May 1995 issue of *Governing.*

Linden's clients have included the National Geographic Society, the Departments of the Navy and Army, Health Data Services, the U.S. Customs Service, the U.S. Department of State, Metro Information

Services, the Cayman Islands government, the chief counsel's office of the IRS, the Department of Justice, the U.S. Information Agency, the FBI Academy, the U.S. Department of Education, two state attorneys general, and more than four dozen other state, local government, and nonprofit agencies.

Before beginning his full-time practice, Linden was a senior faculty member at the Federal Executive Institute. He served as the director of executive programs at the University of Virginia's Center for Public Service, taught at the University of Virginia McIntire School of Commerce, and managed in the human services field for seven years.

Linden earned his bachelor's and master's degrees from the University of Michigan. His Ph.D. is from the University of Virginia.

He lives with his wife and two children in Charlottesville, Virginia.

PART 1

Preparing for Real Change

CHAPTER 1

Overview of Seamless Government Concepts

SEAMLESSNESS DEFINED

Why do I keep buying clothes at Lands' End? They don't offer anything unique. The prices are reasonable but not the lowest. Their policy on accepting returns is fine, but many stores today are as good. The answer is simple. There's no hassle when I call their 800 number. I like what they deliver, and I especially like how easy they make the experience for me. I don't have to wait—I give the operator my order number and VISA number, and the item comes in a couple of days. No extra steps, no forms, no need to give them the same information I've given them dozens of times in the past. I wish I could say that about most hotel chains. (Why, in an age of advanced technology, do so many of them insist on getting my address, the type of car I'm driving, and my phone number when they already have that information in their system?)

Dealing with Lands' End is a seamless experience. It's seamless when I rent a car at Hertz and use my Hertz Gold Club card. Instead of showing the clerk my driver's license and credit card, I just take the airport shuttle and tell the driver my name. The driver checks the computer and drops me off at my rental car, where I often find the motor running, the trunk open, and a form filled out for me.

These aren't stories about technology. They're stories about the power of simplicity, about removing unnecessary steps, about connecting the frontline employee directly with the end user. Many government agencies are learning to provide the same level of seamless service that I have found at Lands' End and Hertz.

Seamless service is effortless service, for both the customer and the provider. Seamless service is characterized by the words *fluid, integrated, connected,* and *transparent* (everything is obvious, and there are no surprises or hidden problems). In a seamless experience, the service provider has a direct connection with the end user, who faces an absolute minimum of forms, approvals, and steps, with no runaround.

"One-stop" shopping has become a popular approach for delivering seamless service today. In the future, we will see many more examples of "no-stop" shopping, in which the end user accesses the information, service, or product without having to stop anywhere (for example, from the user's home computer).

This transformation to seamlessness is already happening in government, as well as in the private sector. Not long ago, a national survey of 800-number users was done to find out which organization has the best, most user-friendly 800 service. The winner? Not L.L. Bean, not Disney, not Nordstrom. No, it was the Social Security Administration. We'll see more public agencies winning such acclaim in the future. This is because consumers have made it clear that they don't care whether they're dealing with a private or public organization—when it comes to service, people today want it "better, faster, and cheaper." And if an organization doesn't deliver, its very livelihood is threatened. That message has gotten through to most government agencies today. To quote Bill Clinton, agencies are "feeling your pain," and many are responding.

Organizations providing seamless service are characterized by the following:

- "Right-to-left" thinking (they begin with desired outcomes and work backward to achieve those outcomes)

- Walls that are replaced by networks (both human and electronic)

- Simple, transparent processes that staff and customers find easy to use

- Multiskilled individuals and teams

- Centralized information and decentralized operations

- A few common principles

An example of moving from a functional to a process orientation is shown in Figures 1.1 and 1.2. Figure 1.1 illustrates a traditional functional organization. Senior management oversees a group of functional departments, such as evaluation, planning, administration, and programs. Figure 1.2 shows the same functional departments, but adds key core and support processes, such as developing new programs and products, delivering programs and products, and providing customer service support.

In organizations like the one illustrated in Figure 1.1, the emphasis is entirely on organizational functions. People with the same background and training work together to produce certain outputs, and they are measured on the basis of those outputs (number of products developed and plans produced, accuracy of budget, number of service calls, and so on). There is nothing wrong with these outputs, of course, but they don't reflect any *outcomes* (results that customers expect from the organization). Outcomes are a key element in organizations like the one depicted in Figure 1.2, where processes are visible. In this instance, staff from the functional departments are loaned to cross-functional teams, which are responsible for outcomes and are measured on factors such as how knowledgeable they are concerning customers' real needs, customer satisfaction with specific programs and services, the speed with which the organization can respond to changing needs, and the like. When employees manage processes, they can be held accountable for real outcomes.

This workbook focuses on the "How?" question—How is it possible to provide seamless service? The book is filled with specific steps, methods, tools, and tips on overcoming barriers. But I'll start with the three fundamental principles critical to providing seamless service:

1. Challenge assumptions

2. Focus on processes

3. Organize around outcomes

PRINCIPLE 1: CHALLENGE ASSUMPTIONS

Assumptions are rarely stated, but they have an enormous power over people's everyday thinking and acting. Common bureaucratic assumptions include the following.

- Division of labor leads to efficiency. (In truth, division of labor leads to dull, narrow jobs that don't tap people's creative abilities. Large, holistic jobs require employees to use judgment and multiple skills; these lead to effectiveness and higher customer value.)

- Multiple layers of review and approval produce greater accountability and control. (In most cases, having many layers of review and approval actually *reduces* accountability and control, because when several people are responsible for ensuring accountability, none of them feels ultimately responsible.)

FIGURE 1.1. A Functional View of the Organization.

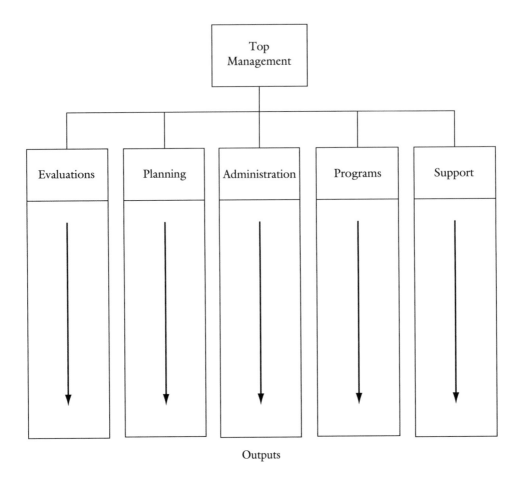

Functional performance criteria:

- Number of products developed and number of studies done

- Number of plans, policies, reports produced

- Budget and personnel policy conformance

- Number of products, programs delivered

- Number of service calls

FIGURE 1.2. A Process View of the Organization.

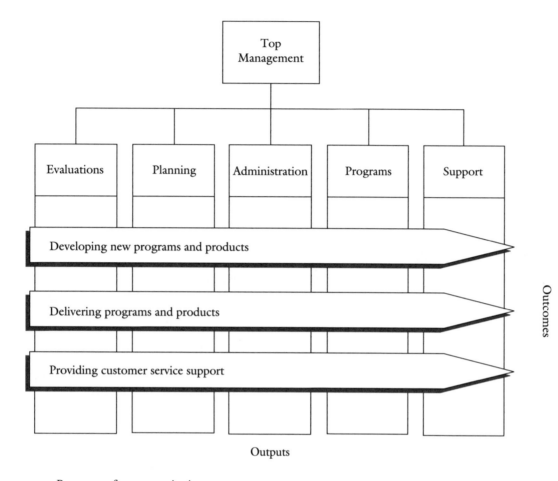

Process performance criteria:

- •Service integration—is it seamless?

- •Knowledge of customer needs—is it accurate?

- •Development of programs and products to meet needs—are customers satisfied?

- •Response time when needs change—is it fast?

- •Reduced costs and higher quality—do customers value these?

- All employees are likely to cheat and make serious mistakes. (This assumption leads to the multiple approvals of most travel and purchase decisions.)
- The conditions that led to this regulation or rule still exist. (Instead, an organization could look at current conditions and determine whether they still necessitate the rule or regulation.)

Seamless service requires us to expose and challenge such assumptions. As we do so, we often find that the assumptions may have been valid in the past but are no longer valid today. And sometimes we learn that they were never valid in the past.

PRINCIPLE 2: FOCUS ON PROCESSES

Organizing along functional lines (for example, accounting, personnel, program offices, budget department, and so forth) made sense in the industrial era, when a stable environment rewarded tight controls. Today's information environment rewards speed, flexibility, integration, and partnerships with suppliers, customers, and other organizations. Success in this environment requires a focus on work processes, not on organizational functions and divisions. That older type of concern only adds to turf battles and slows down work processes.

Processes Defined

Work processes are not always obvious, because most of us have been trained to think about organizational divisions and functions, not processes. What is a *work process*?

A work process is a set of interrelated steps that begin with an input or trigger and end with an outcome that satisfies the end user.

There are two types of processes—core and support. *Core processes* are those that end up touching an external customer; they occur when an employee fills a customer's order, responds to a customer's complaint, or develops a new program or product. *Support processes* are internally focused, such as the process of recruiting, hiring, and trainingnew employees. Here are some core and support processes that are often good candidates for redesign:

CORE (EXTERNAL) PROCESSES	SUPPORT (INTERNAL) PROCESSES
Issuance and collection of parking citations	Purchasing
Inspection process	Recruitment, selection of employees, hiring
Design and construction process	Health benefits claims
Application for classes or services	Employee appeals process
Payment process	Employee recognition process
Accessing information about government services, vacancies, and so forth	Professional development process
	Employee evaluation process
Permit, license processes	Internal audit process
Grant award process	Program evaluation
Development process	Process of issuing work orders
Process of responding to customers' complaints	Budget formulation
New program development	Time and attendance process
Process of planning routes (refuse collection, lawn mowing, and so forth)	Agenda preparation for elected officials' meetings
	Formulating a comprehensive or strategic plan
Tax assessment process	Collecting taxes
Travel process	Managing protective services cases process
	Capital improvement process

Core processes are, of course, the reason an organization exists. Support processes such as budgeting, hiring, and making payments are necessary, but they aren't the purpose of our agencies. (Some internal staff departments still don't understand this fundamental fact. They need to learn it quickly!) Support processes enable the mission-oriented units to do their work. Our organizations exist to satisfy some external, public need, not to process employee payroll, purchase items for the staff, or hire and evaluate them. The agency's external purpose is accomplished by its core processes.

Given that, why spend time redesigning support processes? There are two good reasons. First, we'll never achieve seamless service if we force our employees to deal with rigid, bureaucratic internal processes and systems. The Lands' End operator who does such a wonderful job of filling my order quickly and easily doesn't have to deal with bosses who are monitoring her every movement. On the contrary, she is helped by systems and support staff members who give her the information and responses she needs, when and how she needs them. The second reason to redesign support processes is that doing so sends a very important signal to employees—that the change effort is going to benefit them, not hurt them. Given the number of organizations that have used the word *re-engineering* to mean *downsizing,* it is essential to send positive signals.

PRINCIPLE 3: ORGANIZE AROUND OUTCOMES

When President Kennedy toured Cape Canaveral during the early years of the Apollo moon project, he asked a man sweeping the floor what job he had. The janitor replied, "I'm helping to put a man on the moon." That man understood the ultimate outcome of his and others' efforts.

Unfortunately, his was a rare response. Ask most people what they do at work today and chances are they will describe their *activities:* I'm an accountant, I process payments, I supervise direct-service staff. These may be useful activities, but what's their larger purpose? Many public employees do wonderful work but have no idea how their output contributes to the ultimate outcome. This is one of the problems that seamless service addresses; it focuses people on desired outcomes—the impact and results they are meant to achieve—not on the everyday tasks and activities they perform.

Transforming an organization for seamless service forces us to think about outcomes, about results. That, in fact, is what customers come for; it's what they care about. And that's what we must care about. At the federal government level, the Government Performance and Results Act (GPRA) is forcing most agencies to begin thinking about their desired outcomes. GPRA required almost all federal agencies to have detailed strategic plans in place by October 1, 1997, and those plans are to focus on outcomes, not on inputs and outputs. (GPRA also requires agencies to set annual goals that support their strategic plan, to develop performance measures, and to report on their progress.) Over half of the states have active strategic planning processes in place, as do many local governments. Increasingly, these agencies are distinguishing outcomes—results—from inputs and outputs. And there's a world of difference between the three:

> *Inputs:* information, needs, and problems that trigger an organizational response
>
> *Outputs:* specific programs, products, and services generated
>
> *Outcomes:* the results and impacts of those programs, products, and services

INPUTS	OUTPUTS	OUTCOMES
Number of requests for service	Number of services provided	Percentage of satisfied customers
Number of low-income families needing assistance	Number of families receiving services (food stamps, counseling, and so forth)	Number or percentage of families rising out of poverty
Number of requests for police assistance	Number of arrests	Overall effect on crime level; citizens' perception of safety in their community
Number of enrollees in job training program	Number of classes taught; percentage passing each class	Number or percentage getting and keeping a job for a certain number of years
Number of 911 calls to fire department	Number of fires fought; average response time per fire	Number of deaths or injuries due to fires; amount of property damage due to fires

When staff members focus on their input and output numbers, they are responding to what's usually measured; however, they aren't focusing on their most important task—delivering outcomes. When organizations emphasize, measure, and reward staff for focusing on achieving outcomes, it fundamentally changes the organization's performance. That, for instance, is the real promise of charter schools, which are public schools that receive charters to achieve certain student learning outcomes and that may waive most bureaucratic regulations and rules in their pursuit of those outcomes. And that is the promise and reality of seamless government.

Here are two simple tips on how to identify your desired outcomes:

1. Talk about outcomes with your colleagues. Ask each other, "What *results* are we trying to achieve?" If you hear yourself describing activities (for example, "providing evaluation studies for senior managers," "responding to 911 emergency calls"), you're on the wrong track. Discipline yourselves to articulate the outcomes that such activities should produce. For instance, talk about "ensuring that senior managers can make informed decisions" rather than "producing evaluation studies."

2. Don't assume that you can identify your desired outcomes all by yourselves. It's necessary and enlightening (not to mention scary as hell!) to capture the voice of your customers and other key stakeholders when discussing outcomes. Invite some of them to talk with you about the outcomes you're trying to achieve. Achieving seamless service is largely an "outside-in" process.

NOTE: For a fuller discussion of organizing around outcomes, see Linden, *Seamless Government*, 1994b, pp. 81–93.

OPPORTUNITIES, "SPEEDBUMPS," AND CRITICAL SUCCESS FACTORS IN PURSUING SEAMLESS SERVICE

Benefits

Moving to seamless service provides many opportunities for employees and government's multiple stakeholders. These include the following:

- Improved customer service and customer satisfaction

- Reduced cycle times, which lead to faster service, less waste, less downtime, and better collaboration

- Reduced costs

- Higher quality

- More interesting jobs

- Greater integration of work units

- Closer connections between employees and stakeholders

- Greater public confidence in governmental institutions—confidence that leads to greater support for those institutions and their missions

- An increased sense that work has meaning—meaning that comes from serving others and from connecting with co-workers in a spirit of community

"Speedbumps"

One of my clients, the U.S. Forest Service, is made up of a wonderful, can-do type of folks who typically hate bureaucracy. They love to "get on with it" and do the work they were trained to do. During a workshop at one Forest Service unit, we were discussing barriers to change. One of the managers stood up and said, "Russ, there aren't any barriers here. Barriers are permanent, fixed. You can't get around 'em. What we have are some speedbumps. Speedbumps slow you down. You have to maneuver to deal with them, but they don't keep you from getting where you need to go."

What a great comment! And what a wonderful approach to dealing with problems! Let's identify the major speedbumps to providing seamless service so that we'll know at the outset what problems could arise. The speedbumps could include

- Fighting over turf because people are threatened by the new process design

- Spending a lot of time analyzing the current situation

- Moving forward without strong executive leadership

- Shooting for 5 to 10 percent improvement (which would be incremental, not fundamental, change)

- Failing to communicate throughout the project

- Failing to address employees' concerns

- Staffing the key teams and roles with people who aren't committed to major change, aren't up to the task of leading change, and don't have their supervisors' support to spend time on the change project

- Having trouble focusing on implementation when the environment changes and senior leaders become distracted

- Having difficulty letting go of known, comfortable roles and work relationships

- Having the very people who succeeded in the old approach lead the change

Critical Factors for Success

How can organizational leaders and others deal with these speedbumps? Over the past several years, it has become clear that certain factors promote success:

- Involving senior management continually

- Ensuring that strong, committed people are leading the change effort

- Educating everyone involved to create a common understanding of what seamless service is and isn't, what its payoffs and speedbumps are, and what the general road map is for achieving it

- Capturing the "voice of the customer" throughout the project

- Involving key stakeholders at each phase of the project

- Generating a sense of urgency throughout the change process

- Creating many small and medium-sized steps and engineering early, visible successes

- Not declaring victory too early—persistence is your main ally

- Using just-in-time training (training provided at the time it is needed) for everyone involved

- Understanding that during major change, the perfect is the enemy of the good (the goal isn't a perfect new process or system but a significantly better process or system)

- Communicating . . . and then communicating some more . . . and then some more . . .

Moving toward seamless service isn't rocket science. It takes a lot of common sense and a lot of hard work. And it's worth it.

SUMMARY

In this chapter, I defined *seamless service*. I also discussed three key principles for developing a seamless approach in your agency: challenge assumptions about how and what work is done, focus on processes (not functions and departments), and organize around outcomes (not activities). In addition, I noted the major opportunities and "speed-bumps" involved in the journey toward seamless government, as well as critical factors for getting there.

In the next chapter, I will describe a model for redesigning work.

CHAPTER 2

Preconditions for Major Change

This chapter will introduce a three-phase model for redesigning work processes. Notice that I said "a" model, not "the" model. There is no one model, no "one best way" when it comes to major organizational change. The next time someone tells you that they have "the" model, watch your wallet!

Major change is a complex human endeavor, and there is no formula that applies in all situations. The model described here has worked well for my clients, but only when they understand that they must apply it to their own circumstances and customize it as needed. That's the challenge you face, as well. Use this model as a starting point, not a rigid prescription. Discuss it, ask where it seems to fit your agency's situation and where it needs to be modified, and make it your own. If you do that, it will serve you well.

After I discuss the general model, I will explore its first phase—assessing readiness for major change. I will especially concentrate on one major aspect of this phase—determining whether the key "preconditions" for major change exist in your organization. I will also begin a conversation about managing communications during change projects. This conversation will continue throughout the book, just as it must continue throughout any successful change effort.

THREE-PHASE MODEL

Figure 2.1 reflects the model I use for redesigning work processes. The figure shows a three-phase approach to change: (1) *assessment* (getting ready for change), (2) *design* (planning the changes on paper) and getting senior management agreement, and (3) *implementation* (carrying out the plans). Part One of this workbook explains the assessment phase, Part Two is devoted to the design phase, and Part Three details the implementation phase.

In this chapter, we look at and discuss the importance of using readiness criteria. In the assessment phase, senior leadership determines the organization's readiness for change. I've seen many impatient leaders leap right into the design phase, and that typically leads to disastrous results. The organization may *need* to change, but is it *ready* to do so? If the answer is "Yes," the senior leadership must fill key roles, which are discussed in Chapter Three. The people selected for those roles then meet to begin redesigning the work, and once their designs are approved, they (or another team) implement those designs.

PHASE 1: ASSESSMENT

I will discuss only part of Phase 1 here and will finish the discussion in Chapters Three and Four.

Preconditions for Major Change

Research on many public and private organizational change efforts demonstrates that fundamental change in an organization typically requires the following conditions:

1. *There must be real pain, either current or anticipated.* By *pain,* I mean that people sense a major gap or tension between the way work is done now and the way it must be done in the future. The need for pain may surprise you, given the abundance of books and gurus preaching the importance of *vision* during change. Vision is certainly important, and having a clear strategy is critical to change, but very few organizations manage major change unless its leaders and employees feel dissatisfied with the status quo.

Stating that pain motivates most change isn't a negative comment about human nature. It's a realistic one. In our personal lives, as well as our work lives, we usually need to feel some tension between where we are now and where we want to be in order to make the difficult choice to change. Without that tension, or pain, most people and organizations take the path of least resistance; they maintain the status quo.

FIGURE 2.1. A Model for Redesigning Work Processes.

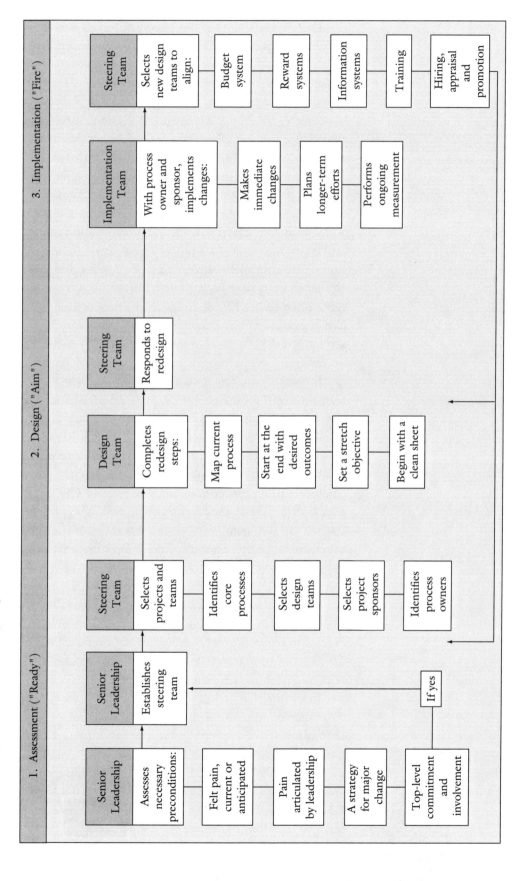

Source: Linden, *Seamless Government,* 1994b. Used with permission.

There are examples of this phenomenon all around us. We change presidents because we're dissatisfied with the current one, not because we love the new candidate. Most people didn't know very much about Ronald Reagan in 1980 when he defeated Jimmy Carter, but they knew they didn't like Carter, so they kicked him out. We change gun control laws after a wave of particularly horrible gun-related violence creates a demand for change. Obese people tend to get serious about dieting and exercise when their bodies rebel and tell them that their overweight condition is causing serious harm (for example, after a heart attack).

In organizational terms, the "pain" or performance gap can come from several sources: a budget shortfall, customer dissatisfaction, competition for resources, difficulty in attracting and keeping talented staff, staff frustration with work processes, outdated technology, competitors who satisfy customers better, or a lack of political support. Many governmental units have begun making major changes in the last several years, often spurred by declining public support for government. When lack of public support translates into declining resource levels, that usually catches the attention of senior leaders and produces a climate ripe for change.

2. *Senior leadership must articulate the pain* in a way that doesn't blame the staff for the problems. Pain, a performance gap, isn't enough to motivate change. The problems must be talked about honestly and openly. The key is to do so without suggesting that the employees are to blame or that all of the employees' past efforts were for naught. Leaders must do the opposite—discuss the gap in a way that motivates employees to seek solutions. As Larry Bossidy, CEO of AlliedSignal, puts it, "I believe in the 'burning platform' theory of change. The leader's job is to help everyone see that the platform is burning." In other words, leaders must show employees that the current way of doing business is leading to a crisis. In Chapter Four, I'll discuss some specific ways in which leaders can do this.

3. *There must be a strategy for change,* an overall plan that describes what all this change is going to accomplish. I often hear managers and executives complain, "My employees just don't see the big picture." There is only one reasonable answer to such a statement: "Has anyone bothered to show them the big picture?"

Employees have had more than enough "flavor of the month" or "management du jour" fads. What they need before making a major change is an honest, credible statement about the *context* for this change. Is it part of a strategy to improve cycle times? To form closer partnerships with suppliers? To involve citizens in identifying problems and opportunities and partnering with them to find and implement solutions? To create more of a team-based culture in order to provide integrated solutions to complex customer needs?

In most agencies today, multiple change projects are going on simultaneously. The leadership challenge here is to paint a picture of the desired future, to describe the basic strategies that will help the organization create that future, and to show how each change project fits into that strategy. As noted earlier, the GPRA is forcing federal agencies to formulate strategic plans, and many states and local governments are doing the same. But the plan means nothing if it becomes "shelfware." It needs to be talked about frankly and directly with employees so that they see where the change is headed, how it may affect them, and how they can contribute. If you do this, their support of the change may amaze you. If you fail to do it, their "wait 'em out" games will kill most change efforts.

4. *Senior leadership must be actively involved,* not just lend verbal support. It's no accident that Dilbert is so wildly popular today. Those clever, biting comic strips hang in most offices, belittling the hair-brained manager who swings from fad to fad without a clue about their meaning. To counteract the cynicism that Dilbert feeds on, leaders can become personally involved in the change effort.

We tend to watch our leaders carefully. One of the ways we judge our leaders' priorities is by noticing the areas to which they devote time and attention. Leaders who announce change but keep a distance from it are sending very clear signals. Leaders who invest time, attention, and energy in a change effort are also sending clear signals.

I've seen dozens of leaders begin a change effort with great intentions. They invest many hours, only to see that investment dwindle as the change became "OBE," or overtaken by events. Employees watch these signs carefully, especially if they have committed to a past effort that went nowhere. The "wait 'em out" game isn't cynical; it's an entirely rational strategy for protecting oneself from further disappointment and wasted time and hope.

Leaders have very few ways to convince employees that a change is for real. One of those ways is to commit large amounts of their own time and energy.

If any of the above four preconditions for major change is not in place, organizational leaders must take appropriate steps. It is unfair to the staff, and it greatly reduces the likelihood of success, if leaders leap into any change project without appropriate preparation.

NOTE: For more discussion of these preconditions for change, see Linden, *Seamless Government,* 1994b, pp. 122–128.

Are you ready for major change? To determine your organization's readiness for change, complete Worksheet 2.1.

WORKSHEET 2.1. Assessing Preconditions for Change.

	YES	SOMEWHAT	NO
1. Existence of real pain, either current or anticipated?	____	_____	____
2. Pain has been articulated by senior leadership?	____	_____	____
3. There is an organizational strategy for change?	____	_____	____
4. Senior leadership is actively involved?	____	_____	____

5. If one or more of the preconditions is not in place, what needs to happen before change begins?

_____

_____

_____

_____

_____

COMMUNICATION AS AN ESSENTIAL PART OF CHANGE

Develop a Communications Plan Now!

The time to think about implementation is *now*, not months later when you have an approved design to implement. People need to be prepared for change, and the best way for them to prepare is to focus carefully on communications throughout the project. Larkin and Larkin (1996) report on a 1993 Wyatt Company survey of 531 U.S. organizations going through major changes. Wyatt asked the CEOs of those companies the following question:

If you could go back and alter one thing about the change effort, what would you change?

Here was the most frequent answer:

The way I communicated with my employees.

Who Should Manage Communications?

It's easy to say, "Pay attention to communications." Of course, but who should do it? To increase your chances of success, senior management should assign responsibility for communications to an individual or team. There are three likely candidates:

1. The project sponsor

2. The design team

3. A separate communications team

NOTE: The project sponsor's and design team's roles are described in detail in Chapter Three.

Project Sponsor

The sponsor, the "champion" of each redesign project, has a good understanding of the project and is often in the best position to communicate to others about the project status. If the project is large and complex, however, the sponsor may have more than enough responsibilities already.

Design Team

The design team (which does the actual work of redesigning a given process) is usually the most enthusiastic about the project, has a great feeling of ownership, and can communicate about the project to others with real intensity and a sense of urgency. Like the sponsor, the design team may be superbusy keeping up with the project. Individual members may be able to contribute to a communications effort, but design teams should usually be allowed to do the design work and not have to take on a major communications role.

Separate Communications Team

A new team is the third option. The team won't have the in-depth knowledge of the project that the sponsor and design team have (but that can be remedied by assigning one design team member to the communications team). Nor will it have the intense feeling of ownership. But it will have time, energy, and a fresh perspective. Moreover, it won't have any of the defensiveness about the project that the design team might feel. Setting up a separate communications team is also a way to involve more people in the change effort.

Good candidates for a communications team are secretaries, people who work in the current process (but who aren't on the design team), internal customers of the current process, and others who want the process changed.

What Should Be Communicated?

It's fine to establish a communications person or group. But what should they talk about? With whom? How often? Here are some tips from past redesign efforts.

- Release some information about the change project every one to three months.

- Describe for other organizational members the status of the design team, the project scope, what's been learned, what they're working on now, what's next in their project, and so forth.

- Highlight interesting facts—customer (dis)satisfaction with the current process, the number of steps in the process, the cycle time for the process, ideas for change, and so forth.

- Post a blown-up map of the current ("as-is") process in a commonly used room in your organization. Publicize the fact that the map is there. Put some paper on the wall next to the map, inviting employees to write comments about the current process.

- Seek input from others in the organization. When information is sent out, seek responses, reactions, advice, and comments. And post those reactions so others can learn from them.

Redesigning work processes can't be managed like the election of a new pope; when that happens, weeks go by while the world waits and watches, and the only sign of progress is the color of smoke coming out of the Vatican meeting hall. Remember: organizations, like nature, abhor vacuums. If you don't put out any information about the project, others will put it out for you, but it will be rumor and misinformation. *You* should get the information out and invite responses.

NOTE: For some tips on the "how" of communications, see Chapter Eleven.

SUMMARY

I introduced a three-part model for redesigning work processes to achieve seamless service, and I emphasized how important it is for you to customize this model to your own circumstances. I also explored the first phase of the model—assessing readiness for change.

Of the four preconditions for major change, one relates directly to the *political* factor. When there is considerable "pain," it can create a powerful constituency for change that will lead the elected officials and political appointees to support change. The second and fourth factors—articulating the pain in a way that doesn't blame the employees, and showing strong leadership involvement—relate to the *people* factor. The other precondition—having an overall strategy for change—is another way of describing the need for a *plan*.

I also introduced the critical element of communications. You can't start thinking about communications too early, just as you can't begin to focus on implementation too soon. I identified three groups that could lead a communications strategy, and I discussed some of the substantive issues that employees want to know about during a major change.

Now it's time to discuss the key people who make change happen. Who does the actual work of changing an organization? Who redesigns the processes, supports this work, and ensures that resources are available to implement the new processes? I will cover the key question of roles in the next chapter.

CHAPTER 3

Key Roles When Redesigning

In the last chapter, I introduced a three-phase model for redesigning work processes and explored part of the first phase, assessment. In this chapter, I will look at the rest of the assessment phase—assigning people to key roles and teams involved in process redesign.

The key roles to be filled during a redesign project include the design team, its leader, subject matter experts, the project sponsor, the steering team, and the process owner. The charter given to the design team must be clear and comprehensive. These points will be discussed below.

DESIGN TEAM

The design team redesigns the way work is done. It takes the current (as-is) process, analyzes it, and comes up with a fundamentally new design.

Design team members must

- Map the current process, identifying bottlenecks, non-value-adding steps, overall cycle time, and satisfaction or frustration with the current process

- Interview end users, those at other agencies affected by the process, and other stakeholders to learn what they need from the process, both today and in the future

- Measure the performance of the current process to establish a baseline

- Benchmark leading organizations to compare their performance with that of the process being redesigned and learn innovative ways to manage the process from the benchmark partners

- Involve subject matter experts, end users, and other stakeholders to gain a full understanding of the process and the possibilities of change

- Recommend a new design to the steering team

- Encourage other staff to support the new process

Most design teams have six to ten members.

NOTE: When redesigning a work process, it is absolutely essential to include both staff members who work in the current process and staff members who are not part of the current process. Those who aren't intimately familiar with the process usually find it easier to get out of the box; they aren't wed to the current process, have no ego or professional identity wrapped up in it, and can ask challenging questions.

TEAM LEADER OR FACILITATOR

The design team needs a leader. Process redesign is challenging enough; the design team shouldn't try to be leaderless or self-managing. The team leader's job is similar to that of a group facilitator. Some redesign projects assign both a team leader and facilitator. This can be especially helpful during the organization's first project, when it is learning how the methodology works and hasn't yet amassed a successful track record.

A team leader must

- Help team members become comfortable with each other

- Develop team-building activities at the start and as needed

- Help the team stay on task, focusing on the methodology and steps

- Identify specific training and technical needs as they arise

- Keep the project sponsor informed of progress and problems

- Help the team identify other people (for example, subject matter experts) who aren't full-time team members but whose expertise and influence would be helpful

- Develop timelines
- Clarify roles
- Ensure follow up on assigned tasks

SUBJECT MATTER EXPERTS

Subject matter experts aren't on the design team, but they are familiar with the process being redesigned and provide specific skills and expertise not available on the team. Subject matter experts are invited to work with the team for a period of time.

Subject matter experts must

- Identify and flesh out ways in which the proposed process will affect information technology, human resources, the budget, and so forth

- Offer specific guidance about technical aspects of the process being redesigned

- Offer help in the use of certain tools (process mapping, quality improvement tools, and so forth)

- Provide guidance in writing an implementation plan

- Help staff members feel that they own the new process by contributing to its design and representing other technical specialists' input

PROJECT SPONSOR

The project sponsor is sometimes a steering team member. He or she should always be a senior organizational member who takes responsibility for a specific redesign project. The sponsor champions the design team's work to the steering team. The sponsor's job is hard to do but simple to state—it is to *see that the design team succeeds.*

The project sponsor must

- Obtain and clarify the charter for design team

- Obtain and allocate resources for the project

- Help identify and obtain high-quality people for the design team

- Represent the design team to the steering team, stakeholders, and others

- Deal with resistance or conflict that the design team encounters

- Support the design team's recommendations to the steering team

- Help the design team set stretch objectives

STEERING TEAM

The steering team is made up of senior people who have major responsibilities for leading the organization. This team doesn't do the redesign work; rather, it oversees all redesign efforts. Because it has such important organizationwide responsibilities, it should include people with broad leadership roles in the organization, such as senior managers who have a general understanding of the processes being redesigned, a union representative (if the agency's employees belong to a union), someone with technical expertise in the processes being targeted for change, and (when possible) a representative of the end users affected by the processes.

The steering team must

- Articulate the need for change and the costs of not changing

- Identify the desired outcomes of the redesign project

- Describe how each project fits into the overall organizational strategy and how each fits in with concurrent change efforts

- Charter and coordinate redesign projects (charters will be described later in this chapter)

- Decide which processes to redesign

- Select project sponsors

- Work with the sponsors to choose design team members

- Decide which design team recommendations to accept

- Ensure that turf concerns do not impede change

- Communicate with key internal and external stakeholders to ensure that they understand the change projects and obtain their input

- Provide resources for the redesign effort and the new process

- Oversee implementation of new process designs

PROCESS OWNER

The process owner is the person with the responsibility and authority to manage the newly designed process. The process owner is a coach and advocate for the process, overseeing and measuring its performance over time and helping to redesign it as needed. The process owner may or may not be the person who currently oversees the process; often, no one person is responsible for the entire process before it changes, which is one reason redesign is needed. The process owner should be on the design team or should meet frequently with it, as this person will have a very big stake in the new design's success.

The process owner must

- Participate on the design team or meet frequently with its members

- Provide technical knowledge as needed

- Stay with the project throughout the design and implementation phases

- Ensure that the proposed ("to-be") design can work and identify issues that need resolution so that the new design can work

- Work with owners of other processes to ensure that the processes are compatible and integrated

The Design Team Has Trouble Getting "Out of the Box"

To help the design team develop creative ideas, take the following steps.

1. Ensure that at least two to three members of the design team are big-picture thinkers with a knack for being creative and innovative.

2. Add two or three members to the team. Do this when the design team is ready to start with a "clean sheet" and begin designing the new process (described in Chapter Nine).

3. Make one design team member the "junkyard dog." I learned this term from U.S. Bureau of Land Management staff members, who find this role essential. They want to make one member responsible for forcing the team to think out of the box. As such, the junkyard dog

Asks wild, outrageous questions.
Continually identifies and challenges the assumptions underlying the current process.
Asks, "Where's the law requiring us to operate this way?"
Asks, "Should the organization be conducting this process in the first place?"

The Design Team Has Trouble Getting Off to a Fast Start
Teams that lack training, clear guidance, and experience working on teams can suffer from the start. In Katzenbach and Smith's wonderful book *The Wisdom of Teams,* they note two significant speedbumps for "teams that recommend things." These speedbumps relate to two times when delays and turf problems often occur: (1) during slow starts and (2) during the handoff from the recommending team to the implementation team (to be discussed in Chapter Twelve).

To help the design team get off to a fast start, give its members a charter that clarifies the team's role, boundaries, goal, and reporting relationships. This is a "no surprises" document that saves both design and steering teams considerable time and frustration.

KEY STEERING TEAM TASK: WRITING A CLEAR CHARTER FOR EACH REDESIGN PROJECT

It is essential that the steering team provide a clear charter for the redesign project. A charter *clarifies the senior leaders' expectations* for the project. It includes

- The process to be re-engineered.

- The importance of fundamentally changing this process.

- The desired outcome of redesigning this process.

- The way this project fits in with the organization's strategy and with other change initiatives.

- The project's scope. (Will the entire process be redesigned? Will the subprocesses that feed into the process also be redesigned?)

- The sponsor's name.

- A recommended time frame for the project.

- An identification of any issues, problem areas, or parameters that the steering team wants the design team to address.

- The way this project fits into an overall strategy for change.

Worksheet 3.1 contains an example of a charter used by the Veterans Affairs Medical Center in Erie, Pennsylvania. In Worksheet 3.2, a blank charter follows.

WORKSHEET 3.1. Comprehensive Care Design Team Charter: Veterans Affairs Medical Center, Erie, PA.

What is the task?	Redesign the continuum of care by eliminating handoffs and optimize information management processes.
Background:	The Executive Leadership Council (ELC) believes that a team with training in Business Process Re-engineering will design a general replacement process of greater efficiency. The ELC thus seeks the team's best recommendations for providing high-quality, high-value patient care in a comprehensive care setting.
Who is giving the task?	The Executive Leadership Council
Who else will be affected by the team's recommendations?	All medical center services and programs
What is the timeline?	
Check in with preliminary report?	_✓_ Yes ____ No
Verbal reports to ELC:	Biweekly
Written reports to ELC:	Monthly
Final report due:	March 29, 1996
Why this timeline is relevant?	The timeline is relevant because we plan to rapidly prototype the team's recommendations for comprehensive care during the second half of FY 1996 and to implement them fully beginning early in FY 1997.
Who is on the team?	Project sponsor: _____
	Process owner(s): _____
Who selects the team leader?	____ Team itself _✓_ Person to whom team reports
Team authority?	_✓_ Offer recommendations ___ Make decisions ___ Implement decisions
Whom to contact for guidance, change in the charter, midcourse check-in, go-aheads when needed?	Conflict resolution, guidance, go-aheads: Process owner Change in the charter, midcourse check-ins: ELC
What are the parameters of the team's project?	Product must be revenue-neutral Laws currently in effect must remain in effect Local policies can be changed VA regulation may be waived
Stretch goals?	Decrease the number of handoffs by 75 percent Decrease the time spent by clinical staff members in recording events by 50 percent

Source: Department of Veterans Affairs Medical Center, Eirie, PA. Used with permission.

WORKSHEET 3.2. Your Design Team Charter.

What is the task?

_____

_____

Why is this task important?
(What is the desired outcome of this project? How
does it fit in with the organization's strategy and
with other change initiatives?)

_____

_____

_____

_____

_____

Who is giving the task?

_____

Who else will be affected by the team's
recommendations?

_____

_____

What is the timeline?

    Should the team check in with a preliminary report? ____ Yes ____ No

    How often should the team submit verbal reports? _____

    How often should the team submit written reports? _____

    What is the due date for the final report? _____

    Why is this timeline relevant? _____

_____

_____

_____

    Who is on the team?

_____

_____

Who selects the team leader?   ____ Team itself   ____ Person to whom
                                                                                team reports

What does the team have the authority to do?   ____ Offer recommendations
                                                                  ____ Make decisions
                                                                  ____ Implement decisions

Whom should the team contact for help when needed (for guidance, change in charter, midcourse check-in, and so on)?

PROBLEM	CONTACT PERSON
Conflict resolution	_____
Guidance	_____
Go-aheads	_____
Change in the charter	_____
Midcourse check-in	_____

What are the parameters of the team's project? (For instance, what options are not OK? What financial and/or legal realities must be honored? What policies must be respected? What political constraints should be considered?)

_____

_____

_____

_____

_____

What is the scope of the project? How far should the team go? (For instance, could this process affect and be affected by other processes? Are other policies involved? Is the process too large to redesign all at once?)

_____

_____

_____

_____

What are the stretch goals?

_____

_____

_____

When will the team get a response to its report?

_____

_____

SUMMARY

This chapter moved from the general to the particular, from broad change concepts to the specifics of roles, tasks, responsibilities, and charters for change. I looked at the key roles of the design team, design team leader, subject matter experts, project sponsor, steering team, and process owner. All of these groups ultimately make a redesign project work. I also described team charters, which are simple tools for reducing surprises and clarifying the "sandbox" within which a design team is free to work.

In terms of the three *p*'s—people, plan, and politics—the charter is a key part of the plan. The various roles to be played relate to the people, of course, but they are also important for managing the politics of change. The political winds may change, budgets may become lean, key stakeholders may change their minds for political reasons, and the relationships among the key teams and individuals may be tested.

The sponsor and steering team leaders have especially important roles. They can act as "downfield blockers" to shield the design team from political problems, so that the team is freed up to do its important work. The steering team is so central to this work that it deserves its own chapter, which I will turn to now.

CHAPTER 4

The Steering Team Takes the Lead

In the last chapter, we looked at the key roles that are needed in a major redesign effort. In this chapter, we will focus specifically on the steering team and its major tasks during the assessment phase. The steering team's overall responsibilities were outlined in Chapter Three. In addition, we will look at five steering team responsibilities: articulating the need for change, identifying the project's desired outcomes, deciding which processes to redesign first, identifying the project sponsor, and selecting the design team members.

ARTICULATING THE CASE FOR CHANGE

The two most frequent questions employees ask when they learn of a major change are

1. Why this change?

2. What's in it for me (sometimes abbreviated as WIIFM)?

Leaders need to anticipate these and similar questions and be ready to give open, honest answers.

Why This Change?

There are several ways in which a leadership team can articulate the need for change and respond to these two questions at the same time. Here are some of the more effective approaches I've seen. Each reflects a major issue that may relate to your organization's environment and situation. The common theme running through each approach is for leaders to cite the "pain" caused by the gap between the way the organization currently works and the way it must begin to work if it is to be successful in the future.

Theme 1: The Customers Are Changing

We've done an excellent job of meeting our customers' needs in the past. Our quality, speed, and service have been good in the eyes of the customer. But the customers' standards are rising. They are becoming better at using technology. They want to do more for themselves and want different contributions from us. The "bar" [standard of excellence] is a moving target, and it's getting higher all the time. So what's worked for us in the past doesn't work so well today. We need to make major changes....

—The head of a state agency information systems unit

Theme 2: The Competition's Improving and We Must Too If We're to Remain Competitive

We've always taken a certain pride that we're the leaders in our area. Unfortunately, we can't say that any longer. We still do a high-quality job, but some of our colleagues in other agencies have gotten faster, smarter, more user friendly, and we don't rate as well as we used to in our customers' eyes. There's no doubt in my mind we're up to the challenge. We can and will make significant changes. We have no choice. If we don't change, our customers will find other providers or do end runs around us. (In fact, some of the larger ones already are doing that.) We no longer have a monopoly....

—The head of a large federal government human resources unit

Theme 3: Everything Is Changing!

It's often said that "the only constant is change." To tell you the truth, I don't like change. I like things the way they are, the way they've been. And maybe I've resisted change too long. But I have no choice any longer.... In fact, we have no choice, because everything is changing:

technology, the employees and their expectations, societal values, the economy, the environment, the competition—everything! We have to radically rethink what business we're in, whom we serve, the roles we'll fill, the way we do our work, even whether we continue to do everything we do today. We have no choice—we have to change.

—The CEO of a large automaker

What's in It for Me?

What most employees want to hear is that their job is secure, that their role will not change, that their identity at work will remain the same. It doesn't make sense to offer such promises. The best response I've heard to this question came from the director of a local government human services agency. She was direct, open, blunt, and caring at the same time. She said:

> I can't guarantee you the same job a year from now that you have today. I'd be lying if I did. I can't guarantee that you'll be in the same work unit or even that you'll be using the exact same skills. What I can tell you is this: the purpose isn't downsizing. The purpose is to get better—much better. Everyone who is willing to "step up," support our effort to change, and be open to new roles and to learning some new skills will have a job. And it won't be a dull, demeaning job. It may feel a bit scary (it does to me, sometimes), but what's scarier is what will happen to all of us if we keep on doing our work the same old way. It just won't cut it.

When her staff heard the message, some of them couldn't handle it and left the agency. A few stayed but fought the change. The great majority, however, took up her challenge, went through an emotional roller coaster for more than two years, and emerged from it stronger and better.

NOTE: We already discussed some methods of communicating these ideas in Chapter Two. There are more tips on communications in Chapter Eleven.

IDENTIFYING DESIRED OUTCOMES FOR THE CHANGE EFFORT

It's important to articulate the need for change. It is just as important to educate staff about the outcomes of the change. For instance, you could tell employees whether you are redesigning certain processes in order to

- Develop faster cycle times for quicker customer service

- Reduce costs

- Improve coordination among separate operational units

- Increase quality

- Develop customized solutions for an increasingly diverse set of customers and stakeholders

As we emphasized in Chapter One, a key principle of redesigning for seamless service is to focus on outcomes, not activities and inputs. Outcomes are best defined in terms of the impact on the ultimate end user. By articulating the desired outcomes of the effort, in terms that relate to end users, the steering team is sending a very powerful message. It is establishing a new way of thinking about work, a way that defines "value added" in terms of impact on end users (rather than on internal organizational activities).

DECIDING WHICH PROCESSES TO REDESIGN FIRST

Once the steering team has articulated the need for change, it must identify the major core and support processes and decide which ones to redesign first. To identify such processes, recall the definition given in Chapter One:

A work process is a set of interrelated steps that begin with an input or trigger and end with an outcome that satisfies the end user.

The steering team should meet with other managers who have thought about redesigning the work. Then, the steering team should review the processes listed in Chapter One and begin listing their own core and support processes. Worksheet 4.1 will guide the steering team in this exercise.

NOTE: Organizations that have gone through this exercise find that they usually identify between five and ten core processes. If you have identified several dozen, you're focusing on subprocesses and "getting into the weeds." Focus on the major, "end-to-end" processes that touch your end users and affect your employees.

The team can use two criteria to select initial processes to redesign. The criteria are

- *Impact* on performance, customers, costs, staff, and the organization's future

- *Feasibility* in terms of costs, external constraints, information technology, and resistance

WORKSHEET 4.1. Identifying Processes That Need Redesign.

1. Brainstorm the organization's major core processes, listing those that directly affect your end users and external stakeholders:

   a. _____   i. _____

   b. _____   j. _____

   c. _____   k. _____

   d. _____   l. _____

   e. _____   m. _____

   f. _____   n. _____

   g. _____   o. _____

   h. _____   p. _____

2. Review the list, checking each proposed process against the definition of process noted above. Which are good candidates for redesign?

CORE PROCESSES

   a. _____   e. _____

   b. _____   f. _____

   c. _____   g. _____

   d. _____   h. _____

SUPPORT PROCESSES (THOSE THAT DIRECTLY AFFECT ORGANIZATIONAL STAFF)

   a. _____   e. _____

   b. _____   f. _____

   c. _____   g. _____

   d. _____   h. _____

Impact

Just because a process is slow and tedious doesn't necessarily make it a good candidate for redesign. Many organizations have radically streamlined a process, only to find that there was little or no impact on overall performance (see Hall, Rosenthal, and Wade, 1993, for examples). The first question to ask is, Which of our processes, if fundamentally improved, would have the biggest impact on our performance and future success?

Here are some questions that the steering team can ask itself and others to determine high-impact processes. Use the processes identified in Worksheet 4.1 when responding to questions 2 through 4:

1. What major challenges will our organization face in the next three to five years?

2. Which processes, if dramatically improved, would give us the agility and responsiveness to meet these challenges and keep up with the demand for continual change?

3. Which processes, if dramatically improved, would make the biggest difference to our current and future end users?

4. Which processes, if dramatically improved, would have a significant impact on our main goals? These goals include

   Implementing the organization's business strategy
   Improving overall performance
   Meeting current and future customer needs
   Attracting and retaining talented staff members
   Responding to important mandates
   Improving quality

Feasibility

The second criterion is feasibility. If a process is terribly hard to redesign, it does little good to identify a process improvement that would delight customers and produce great improvement in performance. Here are some factors that may make some processes less feasible to redesign than others:

- *Cost.* This includes both the cost of immediate changes (for example, the cost of purchasing new technology) and the resulting future costs (for example, the cost of maintaining the new technology).

- *External constraints.* Even if a process needs major change, it may be so constrained by the law, politics, and external constituency groups that oppose any changes that it isn't worth the effort to try.

- *Values and organizational culture.* For instance, academics place a huge value on consensus decision making. As a result, it takes six months to a year or more to fill openings or make policy changes. Many academics would vigorously oppose any attempt to speed up such processes.

- *Managers who control the current process and may or may not support change.* Turf is an issue in virtually all major redesign projects, of course, and it must be addressed. For the first project, however, you may want to select processes controlled by managers who clearly favor major change and who are eager to receive help in making such change.

- *Status of current and planned information technology.* How old are your current systems? What has been planned for the next one to three years? Has money been programmed for new systems? Can certain processes only be changed through a major investment in new technology?

Once you have debated these questions, you are ready to select processes for the initial redesign projects. The grid in Worksheet 4.2 can help you sort out your major core and support processes. Place each process you identified in Worksheet 4.1 in the grid, based on your assessment of (1) the likely impact that major improvements would have on the process and (2) the feasibility of making such improvements.

Once you sort the processes using this grid, you can examine the implications. Two are immediately clear.

- Processes identified as "high impact, high feasibility" are clear winners. Not many processes fall into this category, but those that do are what golfers call "gimmes." They're automatic winners.

- Processes considered to be "low impact, low feasibility" are also "no-brainers." There's no reason to spend time redesigning them.

The less obvious processes, then, are in the other two cells.

- If your process is "low impact, high feasibility," it won't change the world if you improve it. But your chances of successfully changing it are very good. Plus, going through with the change will teach you and your teams a great deal about redesign methodology and team roles. You'll also send a clear signal to the troops by starting with a winner. Some organizations select one such process in the first redesign effort for this very reason.

WORKSHEET 4.2. Deciding Which Processes to Redesign.

Given your responses to this matrix, which processes do you select to redesign?

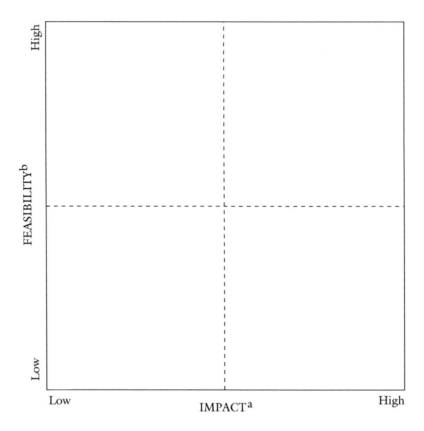

[a]The effect on external customers, staff, performance, costs, and so forth.

[b]The ease or speed of implementation.

- What about processes that are "high impact, low feasibility"? Many government processes fall into this category. Improving such processes takes a long time, sustained effort, committed leaders, and often more than a little money. It doesn't make sense to start with two or three processes such as this, because the chances of success aren't high. However, it may be useful to include one such process in the first or second redesign effort to show the staff that you're serious about major change and that you're "going after the big ones."

SELECTING THE PROJECT SPONSOR

The choice of project sponsors is critical, and the steering team needs to give it careful consideration. I've seen strong sponsors save projects that were otherwise going south, and I've seen some sponsors take a hands-off approach that caused continual delays and frustration for the design team.

The sponsor isn't involved in all design team meetings. He or she comes periodically but stays in close touch with the team leader. The sponsor helps anticipate problems and acts as a "downfield blocker" to remove problems and resistance that would only distract the team.

Who can play this role? Here are some characteristics to seek in project sponsors:

- Determination to make the project succeed

- Creativity

- Political skills (in the sense of reading people well, relating well to leaders, being able to marshal support for good ideas, dealing with others' concerns tactfully, communicating well, and being respected for past successes)

- Abundant energy

- Good interpersonal skills

- Credibility (which is perhaps most important)

Along with these characteristics, the steering team should consider the tasks a sponsor must perform (see Chapter Three). Before selecting a sponsor, the steering team should ask itself this question: "Of the candidates for sponsor, who has the time, credibility, and interpersonal skills that will inspire confidence in us and in others?" With these considerations, the steering team can select a sponsor for each redesign project.

CHOOSING DESIGN TEAM MEMBERS

Before assigning or inviting people to join design teams, consider the following characteristics of an effective design team:

DESIGN TEAM CHARACTERISTICS

- Has six to ten people

- Includes some who perform the process and some who do not

- Includes people who can disagree candidly and who are willing to look for consensus

- Has some members who are able to get out of the box and think very creatively

- Has members who are willing to commit to the project's success and who are not wed solely to defending their own department's turf

- Has members who are respected by others

- Includes some people who understand the technical aspects of the process (for example, aspects affected by legal, regulatory, policy, financial, and/or technical considerations)

- Includes people from human resources and information systems units, if necessary

With these characteristics in mind, the steering team or sponsor (or both) can select members for the design team. Worksheet 4.3 should help in this endeavor.

Some Supervisors Don't Give Staff Members Time and Support to Serve on Design Teams When a redesign project begins, supervisors and managers are generally supportive. But as the project moves along, some supervisors start to resent the time their staff spend at design team meetings. Most redesign projects of any size require at least one day a week for design team work, and they frequently require more than that. Design team members need the support of their supervisors. They need relief from some of their projects and priorities. When supervisors don't provide such relief, the staff members suffer, the redesign project suffers, and ultimately the organization suffers.

When Appraising Supervisors' Performance, Consider Their Support of Redesign Efforts The steering team can take a big step toward ensuring the project's success by making it clear to all that the change effort is an organizationwide priority. And the

WORKSHEET 4.3. Choosing Design Team Members.

Process to be redesigned (from Worksheet 4.2):

1. Brainstorm names of possible design team members.

a. _____	i. _____
b. _____	j. _____
c. _____	k. _____
d. _____	l. _____
e. _____	m. _____
f. _____	n. _____
g. _____	o. _____
h. _____	p. _____

2. Look again at the design team tasks (Chapter Three) and characteristics of ideal design team members (Chapter Four). Which ten people best fit these criteria? Put an asterisk next to their names in the above list.

3. The project sponsor should invite at least six of the people identified in the previous step to join the team, after seeking their supervisors' support. The sponsor should then inform the steering team of the final list.

4. List the names of six design team members.

a. _____

b. _____

c. _____

d. _____

e. _____

f. _____

team can make that priority a reality by emphasizing it in evaluations of supervisors who lend staff to the effort. It's often said that "what gets measured gets managed." If leaders measure the support given by their managers and supervisors, that support will be forthcoming.

ASSESSING WHETHER YOU ARE READY TO MOVE ON

Worksheet 4.4 summarizes the key tasks that you need to complete before moving on to the design phase. The steering team, project owner, and design team leader should review this checklist to determine whether everything is in place. If it is, you can begin the core activity of the project—redesigning the work.

SUMMARY

This chapter detailed five important steering team responsibilities during the assessment phase: articulating the need for change, identifying the project's desired outcomes, deciding which processes to re-engineer first, identifying the project sponsor, and selecting the design team members.

In three of these early activities, the steering team deals with the *people* part of change when it makes a compelling case for change, selects the design teams, and fills the sponsor roles.

The steering team also makes a strategic decision when it selects one or more processes to be redesigned. This decision completes the *plan* for getting started; now it is clear *why* the organization is changing, *who* is doing the changing, *when* the change is to begin and end, and *what* is to change.

These decisions and activities also bear on the *politics* of change. When a change method is introduced for the first time in an agency, few people will have had any experience with it. How do they decide if it's good for them and for the agency? One way is by observing who has been put in charge of the project. When those selected for project sponsor and design team roles are respected for their technical and management skills, it sends a signal about senior management's commitment. Others begin to show enthusiasm and willingness to contribute. And it positions the organization to begin the exciting work of actually redesigning work processes.

Chapters Two, Three, and Four have covered the major tasks in the assessment phase. Next comes the most exciting part of the change process—the actual redesign of the work itself. We turn to that in the next chapters.

WORKSHEET 4.4. Are You Ready to Move On?

Members of the design team should work with their sponsor to determine whether the following tasks have been accomplished:

Team members have been selected.

_____

A team leader or facilitator has been selected.

_____

Team members have been given ample time away from their jobs to complete the project. (This must be agreed to by team members' supervisors. If there is a problem, the sponsor needs to get involved with those supervisors and, if necessary, needs to consult the steering team.)

_____

A project sponsor has been selected.

_____

A process owner has been identified.

_____

The process to be redesigned has been selected.

_____

A charter has been prepared.

_____

A design team has been taught the principles and methods of redesigning processes. They also know about team dynamics.

_____

A communications plan is in place.

_____

2

Redesigning Your Work Processes

CHAPTER 5

Four Steps to Redesigning Key Processes

ONE BELIEF AND FOUR KEY STEPS

Once you have assessed your organization's readiness for change, created a communications plan, and filled the key roles, you are ready for the design phase, in which the analysis and design of your processes take place. A number of tools and techniques will help you during the phase. These are detailed in the following four chapters. However, one fundamental aspect of this change method has nothing to do with tools and quantification. It is one of the principles mentioned back in Chapter One. Design teams must always be ready to *surface and challenge the assumptions about the way the work is done, even about whether certain work should be done at all.*

Many people are so familiar with their current processes that they find it difficult to think out of the box and to challenge assumptions. Thus, it is critical to get help from others. To identify the assumptions underlying the current process, ask customers, suppliers, and staff from other units to look at your process and to help you identify those assumptions. Force yourselves to ask a question that management guru Peter Drucker asked more than twenty years ago:

If we weren't already in the businesses we're currently in, would we get into them today?

Drucker urged managers to challenge the most fundamental assumption—whether they should be doing certain work at all. Public sector managers can translate Drucker's classic question as follows:

If we weren't already running our current programs and services, would we begin each of them today?

To answer this question honestly takes some confidence, security, guts, and a willingness to embrace change. That's what you need when redesigning your work for seamless service. It starts with a willingness to question assumptions. Remember: most assumptions are so basic that they become part of the landscape and we take them for granted. Be ready to surface and identify your assumptions. Be ready to challenge them.

FOUR STEPS FOR REDESIGNING A PROCESS

There are four major steps in the design phase:

- Map the current process

- Establish the desired outcomes

- Set a stretch objective

- Design from a clean sheet

These four steps are explored in the following four chapters. Figure 5.1 also shows them in more detail.

FIGURE 5.1. The Design Phase Steps.

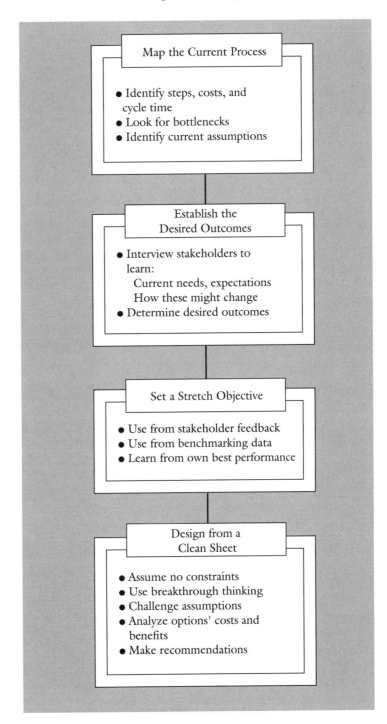

CHAPTER 6

Mapping the Current Process

FIGURE 6.1. Four Steps for Redesigning a Process.

1. Map the current process
2. Establish the desired outcomes
3. Set a stretch objective
4. Design from a clean sheet

PURPOSE OF MAPPING THE CURRENT PROCESS

It is important to understand your processes before you change them. Mapping the current process can provide several benefits. Such a map

- Provides a baseline of current performance, helping the team determine whether its new process is an improvement

- Portrays how the entire "end-to-end" process actually works

- Identifies some immediate opportunities for reducing non-value-added steps, waiting time, frustration and bottlenecks, overlap and redundancy

- Is a communications tool; it involves people, helps them see the need for change, and builds confidence in the overall redesign effort

- Generates increased commitment for change, because the map makes the "pain" of the current process so evident

OUTCOMES OF THIS STEP

Once the design team has completed its map of the as-is process, it will have three important outcomes:

1. A graphic portrayal of the current process, one which is understandable and accessible to all

2. An awareness of why the process needs to be changed and an increased desire to change it

3. A consensus about the process's desired outcomes

HOW TO MAP THE CURRENT PROCESS

Here are the substeps involved:

1. Identify the people who currently perform the process.

2. Interview those people to determine the following:

    The steps and substeps of the process
    The average processing (work) time required to complete each step
    The amount of waiting time in which nothing moves the process forward

The total cycle time (start to finish) for the whole process
The steps that are especially frustrating to perform

3. Prepare a visual map of the current process.

4. Identify assumptions on which the current process is based.

5. Determine whether you are ready to move on to the next design step.

We'll discuss each step in detail.

1. IDENTIFY THE PEOPLE WHO CURRENTLY PERFORM THE PROCESS

This step may seem unnecessary, but it's not always obvious who performs the process. Indeed, one frequent result of mapping the current process is that it uncovers all kinds of surprises and opportunities. One opportunity is to clarify who actually does the work.

Start with the managers who are responsible for the process and ask them who works on the process on an ongoing basis. Then contact each of those employees, find out how they contribute to the process, and ask them who else works on the process. When you start hearing the same names repeated, you'll know you have a good starting list of employees.

2. INTERVIEW THOSE PEOPLE TO LEARN HOW THE PROCESS WORKS

The process analysis sheets in Worksheets 6.1 and 6.2 give you a way to record information about the current process. The example in Worksheet 6.1 is from a team that redesigned the zoning and special use permits process in Prince William County, Virginia. The team learned that there were nine major steps in the process. They used this tool to determine the processing time, waiting time, cycle time, and level of staff frustration in performing the process. Worksheet 6.2 is a blank version of Worksheet 6.1. With the blank form, you can examine how the current process works in your organization. You should use this tool when interviewing employees who perform the process. This is the first substantive step in mapping the current process.

WORKSHEET 6.1. Sample Process Analysis Sheet.

Step	Staff processing time	+	Waiting time	=	Total step time	Cycle time (Cumulative)	Staff frustration
1. Preapplication conference							H M (L)
2. Application submission, quality control	1		13		14	14	H (M) L
3. Agency review	2		19 – 33		21 – 35	35 – 49	H (M) L
4. Summary letter	5		9 – 37		14 – 42	49 – 91	H (M) L
5. Issue resolution, final submission	8		13 – 90		21 – 98	70 – 189	H (M) L
6. Staff report	5		16		21	91 – 210	(H) M L
7. Planning commission hearing	1		13		14	105 – 224	H (M) L
8. Staff report	1		15 – 29		16 – 30	121 – 254	(H) M L
9. Board hearing	1		11		12	133 – 266	H (M) L
Totals	24		109 – 242		133 – 266	133 – 266	

Source: This example comes from Prince William County, Virginia. Used with permission.

Note: Numbers represent days.

WORKSHEET 6.2. Your Process Analysis Sheet

Step	Staff processing time	+	Waiting time	=	Total step time	Cycle time (Cumulative)	Staff frustration
							H M L
							H M L
							H M L
							H M L
							H M L
							H M L
							H M L
							H M L
							H M L

Here is an explanation about how to fill out Worksheet 6.2.

Step

In the first column, write down the steps that take place in the current process.

Staff Processing Time

In the second column, record the total number of hours employees spend performing each step.

Waiting Time

Ask the staff how much time passes during each step when no work is being done on the specific task. This isn't about laziness. It's about the amount of time during which no work can be done because the process is set up that way. Perhaps a form is sitting in someone's "in" box. Maybe an approval is needed, and the approval process usually takes three days. Perhaps someone must review the step, which often requires one week. Whatever the reason, record in the third column the amount of waiting time encountered in each step of the process.

Total Step Time

In the fourth column, add up the number of hours or days you wrote in the second and third columns. Use Worksheet 6.1 as a guide.

Cycle Time

In the fifth column, you must find a cumulative number. For the first row, put the same number that you have for "Total Step Time." For each subsequent step, take the "Cycle Time" number from the previous row and add it to the number shown in "Total Step Time."

Staff Frustration

Ask those who currently perform the process to estimate their level of frustration when performing each step. Is it high, medium, or low? Note that this is *not* the frustration that the customers of the process experience; you will interview and survey customers later to determine that. Depending on the answer, circle H, M, or L in the last column to show the average response from the employees interviewed.

3. PREPARE A VISUAL MAP OF THE CURRENT PROCESS
Use a Box Flow Chart or a Functional Flow Chart

There are several ways to construct a visual map of a work process. Some people prefer very sophisticated modeling tools, the most popular being IDEF (short for Integrated Definition), a computer-aided tool developed by the air force that provides a structured analysis of all business activities, their relationships, and the flow of information supporting the activities. For more on IDEF modeling, see Appleton (1994).

For most processes, however, I prefer a simple visual representation of the major steps. Why? Because I've seen many teams invest several months trying to model the current process perfectly, often leading to lost time and energy and a depleted ability to develop new ideas for change.

Thus, most teams do well using a simple mapping tool such as a box chart or functional flow chart. Which one of those two should you use? It depends on the complexity of the process you're trying to map and the amount of information you need to understand in order to redesign it. If the process is reasonably straightforward, with few decision points, steps, and handoffs, then the box flow chart may suffice. A sample box flow chart appears in Worksheet 6.3, again using the Prince William County rezoning and special use permit process to illustrate the concept. In Worksheet 6.4, there is space for you to construct your own box flow chart. This tool allows you to see the sequence of major steps in a process, as well as the time frame involved.

To create a box flow chart, you need to do the following:

1. Take the steps you identified in the first column of Worksheet 6.2 and write each one in a separate box, putting the boxes in order.

2. Indicate the average amount of time spent on each step (for both working *and* waiting) and put that number in the box.

3. Show the cumulative amount of time for the steps by adding the time required for the step to the time elapsed during all previous steps.

The box flow chart is clearly helpful for a process as simple as the one in Worksheet 6.3. But if you have a large process that crosses two or more organizational lines and involves several decision points, it warrants a functional flow chart. This more detailed tool is especially helpful in pointing out the redundancies, delays, non-value-adding steps, and turf problems created by a process that crosses two or more organizational boundaries.

In Worksheet 6.5, there is an example of a functional flow chart from a large department of public works. The chart reflects the process that this organization used to obtain grading permits prior to reengineering. Worksheet 6.6 has space for you to create your own functional flow chart.

WORKSHEET 6.3. Sample Box Flow Chart.

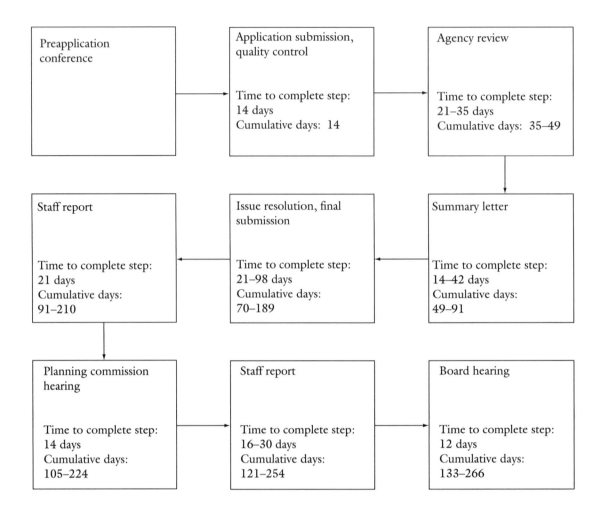

WORKSHEET 6.4. Your Box Flow Chart.

WORKSHEET 6.5. Sample Functional Flow Chart.

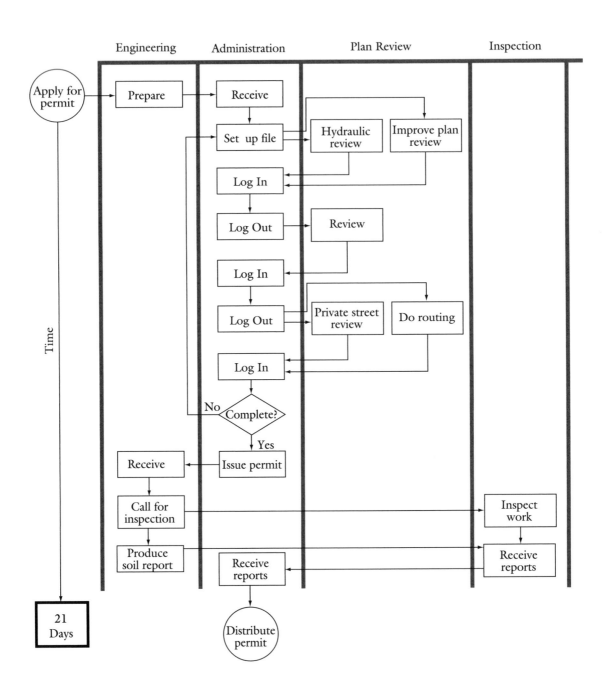

WORKSHEET 6.6. Your Functional Flow Chart.

Time

To create a functional flow chart, you need to do the following:

1. Look at the steps you identified in Worksheet 6.2.

2. Identify the functions (departments, divisions, or units) in which each step takes place.

3. Write the names of those functions along the top of the horizontal axis on the functional flow chart. (For example, engineering, administration, plan review, and inspection are the functions listed in Worksheet 6.5.)

4. Beginning with the input or activity that triggers the process, put every step on the flow chart. Starting at the upper left, use a rectangle for action steps, a diamond for decision points, and a circle or oval for the beginning and ending steps in the process. Put every step in a column under the appropriate function.

5. Along the vertical axis, show the elapsed time needed to perform the process.

NOTE: Before you move on, validate your process map with those who perform the process.

Once you have the basic information about the process (steps, cycle time, frustration, and so forth), take a little time to validate it with some of those who perform it. You don't need to review it with everyone who gave you input, and the process doesn't have to be "perfect." But the design team will gain credibility and build consensus for change if you check in with a sample of those who work in the process to ensure that the map is accurate in its basic outline.

The Design Team Spends Too Much Time Mapping the Current Process I've seen it over and over. The design team tries to get the map of the process perfect. Then, it spends more time developing another level of detail. Subsequently, it tries to map some of the major variations of the process. Next, it tries using some powerful mapping software, and so on. The desire to make it perfect typically creates far more problems than it solves. The team wastes time and energy. And the more the design team learns about the minute details of the process, the harder it is to be creative when it's time to redesign the process.

Create a Good Map of the As-Is Process and Move On There's a saying on Washington's Capitol Hill that serves us well here:

The perfect is the enemy of the good.

There is no "perfect" bill in Congress, because the art of making a bill into law is just that—an art. It involves trade-offs, back-scratching, and compromise. Those who insist on waiting for a perfect bill might as well go to the closest cemetery and wait. . . . The perfect bill ain't coming! The goal in Congress is a good bill. And that's our goal at this point—a good process map.

We need to manage expectations during a major change effort, and if the design team expects itself to be perfect, others will assume the same expectations, to the detriment of all. How much information do you need about the as-is process? Just enough to get a general understanding of its time, costs, frustrations, positive aspects, output and outcomes, and opportunities for change. Once you have that, you're ready to move on.

4. IDENTIFY ASSUMPTIONS ON WHICH THE CURRENT PROCESS IS BASED

We've already discussed the importance of identifying and challenging assumptions. Here are some common bureaucratic assumptions:

- Each step must be completed before the next one can begin.

- Every employee is likely to cheat or make a mistake.

- Multiple approvals mean greater accountability and control.

- The process must be performed the same way every time (one size fits all).

- If each unit achieves its own objectives, the entire organization will succeed.

Many of these assumptions appear in Worksheet 6.5, which charts an old process in a department of public works. Obtaining grading permits involved at least five different approvals, reflecting an assumption that numerous approvals provide accountability and control. It was a classic one-size-fits-all process—every applicant went through the same steps, whether the application was risky or simple. (This happened even though a study of the process revealed that 40 percent of the applicants for grading permits didn't even need a permit!) As many as fifteen different specialists worked to approve the permits, which reflected an assumption that every application posed challenging problems that only well-trained specialists could solve. (In truth, only 25 percent of the applicants had complicated situations.)

The team that redesigned this process challenged these assumptions and came up with a dramatically different and better way of working (which appears later in this book in Worksheet 9.2). The new process is based on these changed assumptions:

- Multiple approvals don't add up to accountability and control. If everyone is accountable, nobody really is. One point of responsibility is appropriate.

- One size doesn't fit all. Instead, applicants with different needs should go through different processes. (This is what the hospital world calls "triage," or sorting the customers according to needs and conditions.)

- Most applications are not complex and risky. Thus, a few well-trained generalists can handle most applications and can also determine which applications do need specialists' attention.

How to Identify Assumptions in a Process

Imagine for a moment that an agency was embarrassed fifteen years ago when it issued a policy that contradicted another agency policy. A senior manager was roasted in the media for the mistake, and he decided never to go through that again. His solution? Whenever the agency wrote a new or revised policy, every agency division would review and possibly change or veto the proposed policy. This solution was implemented and it achieved the desired goal; there were no more public embarrassments. The cost of this solution? It took an average of nine months to produce policies that could easily have been developed in three months or less.

A rare example? Unfortunately not! In fact, this is a classic case of a common government problem: few are guilty, but all are punished. Because one problem happened once and someone was embarrassed, the organization makes wholesale changes that are entirely centered on avoidance. We can spend our entire week avoiding problems, but what do we accomplish?

Worksheets 6.7 and 6.8 show how to identify the assumptions in your process. Worksheet 6.7 is a sample version of Worksheet 6.8; the two pose the same questions, and Worksheet 6.7 answers them for the government agency that seeks to avoid public embarrassment.

Clearly, there are alternatives to the tedious policy-making and policy review process that Worksheet 6.7 reflects. One would be to use "triage," separating the complex policies from the simpler ones. Another would be to gather staff members from the divisions affected by a proposed policy and to hold a meeting in which they discuss the policy. This is preferable to the way employees prolong the process by passing memos back and forth, arguing over each point. Many other options are also available, and they become more obvious as the process's underlying assumptions are explored and debated.

WORKSHEET 6.7. Sample Process Assumptions.

1. What are the major problems with the current process, as the design team sees it?

    a. The policy review process takes far too long.

    b. It ties up too many people's time.

    c. The process often leads to poorly written, unintelligible policies, because they tend to be written piecemeal as each division reviews and edits them.

2. What rules, written and unwritten, seem to be involved with one or more of these problems?

    a. The stated rule: every division exercises a potential veto over each proposed policy.

    b. The unstated rule: those involved in policy-making should check frequently with their bosses, which slows things down to a crawl and puts no real authority or responsibility in the hands of the policy writers.

3. Is there a relevant history to any of these rules?

    The agency was publicly embarrassed when it issued a new policy that contradicted an old one. Since then, the agency has insisted that every proposed policy go through an endless round of checks.

4. Given the rules and the history, what assumptions underlie this process? In what way are these assumptions true or false?

    a. Every proposed policy relates to all organizational units. (In fact, a minority of the policies relate to the whole organization.)

    b. All proposed policies are highly complex; no single staff member can understand the implications of a policy. (True in some cases, but not true for most.)

    c. One size fits all. All policy development must be handled in an identical fashion.

    d. It isn't important to turn around work quickly. Avoiding any error is the highest good.

WORKSHEET 6.8. Your Process Assumptions.

1. What are the major problems with the current process, as the design team sees it?

 a. _____

 b. _____

 c. _____

2. What rules, written and unwritten, seem to be involved with one or more of these problems?

 a. _____

 b. _____

 c. _____

3. Is there a relevant history to any of these rules?

 _____

 _____

 _____

 _____

4. Given the rules and the history, what assumptions underlie this process? In what way are these assumptions valid or not valid?

 a. _____

 b. _____

 c. _____

 d. _____

 e. _____

 f. _____

Save Worksheet 6.8 after you have identified the assumptions in your process. Having this sheet will help you when you reach the fourth design step—redesigning the process from a clean sheet.

5. DECIDE WHETHER YOU ARE READY TO MOVE ON TO THE NEXT DESIGN STEP

The purpose of mapping the as-is process is to produce an accurate picture of the process and its current performance. You are ready to move on if your team can answer yes to the questions in Worksheet 6.9.

SUMMARY

This chapter examined the steps for mapping and analyzing your current process. The steps are based on the assumption that you need to understand your work processes before you can change them.

The primary *people* involved in mapping your processes are the design team and those who perform the processes. The *plan* for doing this work is straightforward: determine who currently works on the process, interview those people to learn how the process works, develop flow charts and analyses of the process's steps (showing cycle time, waiting time, and so forth), and identify the assumptions on which the process is based.

Following these steps will help you deal with the *politics* of change in two ways. First, you've listened carefully to a group that has a vested interest in the process—the staff members who perform it every day. Second, you've put together a flow chart and analysis that clearly portray the "pain" caused by the process. This, together with considerable input from the process's end users, will help reduce resistance from those invested in the current process and will make a strong case for change.

To discuss the end users' views of the process further, I will move on to the next step in redesign—establishing desired outcomes. This will be the topic of Chapter Seven.

WORKSHEET 6.9. Are You Ready to Move On?

1. Do others validate the map as accurate?   _____

2. Do you have baseline information about the process's performance (number of steps, cycle   _____
time, processing time, bottlenecks, and staff frustration)?

3. Is your flow chart understandable? Could those who don't work in the process understand
it from the steps you've outlined?   _____

4. Have you identified the assumptions on which the process is based?   _____

5. If you answered no to any of the above, what do you have to do to complete this phase?

_____

_____

_____

_____

_____

CHAPTER 7

Establishing Desired Outcomes

FIGURE 7.1. Four Steps for Redesigning a Process.

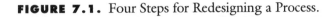

1. Map the current process

2. Establish the desired outcomes

3. Set a stretch objective

4. Design from a clean sheet

PURPOSE OF ESTABLISHING DESIRED OUTCOMES

In Chapter One, we discussed three essential principles in designing processes for seamless service. One of the principles is to organize around outcomes—results—not activities, inputs, or even outputs. By this point in the effort, the senior managers on the steering team should already have identified the desired goal of the organizationwide change. The design team needs to articulate more specific outcomes that relate to the particular process being improved.

OUTCOMES OF THIS STEP

Once the team completes this step, it will have one or more clearly stated outcomes to achieve. In addition, it will have identified the key stakeholders' needs and their expectations of the process. Finally, the stakeholders will feel involved in the redesign effort.

HOW TO START AT THE END WITH DESIRED OUTCOMES

There are several substeps involved here:

1. Identify key stakeholders.

2. Choose a way of learning about stakeholders' needs and expectations.

3. Interview or survey stakeholders to determine desired outcomes.

4. Compare and analyze data from stakeholders, synthesizing desired outcomes.

5. Communicate the results to key stakeholders.

6. Decide whether you are ready to move on to the next design step.

Don't Reinvent the Wheel There is no need to survey customers and other stakeholders if they have recently been surveyed. Most customers have filled out far too many surveys, and far too little has changed as a result. Similarly, there is no reason to gather data on the process if that has been done recently.

Find out what information has been gathered on stakeholders before jumping into this step. Federal agencies are required to have much of this information in order to comply with GPRA. Many other governmental units gather similar information when they do strategic planning.

You'll save some time by checking recent studies of stakeholders; you'll also avoid alienating them if they were in fact recently surveyed.

1. IDENTIFY KEY STAKEHOLDERS

The design team begins by brainstorming a list of external and internal stakeholders. Worksheet 7.1 is a good place to record this list. The team should consult with its sponsor or steering team to ensure that every important stakeholder has been included on the list. What is a stakeholder? Here's how Bryson and Alston, 1996, define it:

A stakeholder is an individual or group that can influence the organization's direction, that is influenced by the organization, or that can make a claim on its resources or direction.

The design team should discuss this initial list of stakeholders. Then, using Worksheet 7.2, the team should determine a final list of stakeholders to be included in this phase of the project. If the team identified a relatively small number of stakeholders (say three to six), it may want to survey or interview all of them. If it has identified a large number of stakeholder groups, though, it may have to decide which to contact and which to skip, depending on the amount of time available. Before moving to the next step, the team should consult with its sponsor on its final stakeholder list.

 **Not All Stakeholders Can Be Approached Directly** Some stakeholders may be very important to the agency but "off-limits" to the design team in terms of direct contact. For instance, most federal agencies consider Congress (or its relevant committees) to be a key stakeholder; typically, however, a design team won't have the authority to approach congressional members directly to obtain their input on process changes.

 **Use Your Sponsor** The design team has a sponsor for just this kind of issue. Ask the sponsor whom you can approach directly. In a federal agency, for instance, it's usually the Office of Congressional Affairs that would deal with members of Congress.

2. CHOOSE A WAY OF LEARNING ABOUT STAKEHOLDERS' NEEDS AND EXPECTATIONS

There are three general ways to learn about stakeholder needs and desired outcomes: surveys, focus groups, and individual interviews.

External stakeholders

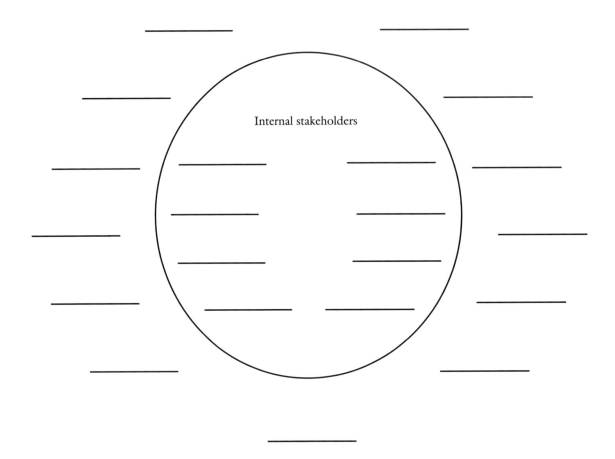

Internal stakeholders

Source: Bryson and Alston, 1996. Used with permission.

WORKSHEET 7.2. Stakeholder Selection.

Which stakeholder groups do you feel are necessary to contact? Some stakeholders will be more important than others because of their size, their clout, their past relationship with your agency, their critical role concerning your mission, the relative importance of their needs, and so forth. List the important stakeholders here:

_____

_____

_____

_____

_____

_____

_____

_____

_____

_____

_____

Surveys

Advantages

Surveys provide an efficient way to gather lots of data fairly quickly. They allow input from many people. They also provide easily quantified data that are more valued in some organizations than are "soft" data from focus groups and interviews.

Disadvantages

Surveys don't allow deeper examination or follow-up to learn the reasons for a person's response. Nor can the respondent raise issues not identified in the survey questions or react to other respondents' ideas (as is possible in focus groups).

Focus Groups

Advantages

Focus groups are structured interviews with groups of six to twelve people. They provide in-depth, qualitative information about stakeholder needs and expectations. They have the advantages provided by face-to-face interactions: the facilitator can follow up on specific questions, probe for deeper levels of understanding, and read body language as an additional clue to participants' attitudes. In addition, focus group participants react to one another, thus providing information that might not emerge from individual interviews or surveys.

Disadvantages

Focus groups are not efficient; it typically takes an hour and a half or more to obtain information from a relatively small group of participants. Furthermore, they do not easily lend themselves to quantification; thus, their results must be interpreted by those who conduct them.

Individual Interviews

Advantages

There may be stakeholders who are critical to the success of the redesigning project, whether because of their role in the process being redesigned, because of their power in the organization, or for other reasons. Some stakeholders should be interviewed individually, rather than included in a focus group. Individual interviews can keep these key stakeholders' views separate and give those stakeholders the attention they expect.

Disadvantages

Individual interviews are even more time consuming than focus groups. Plus, interviewing one or a few stakeholders may send a negative message; others could feel that some people's responses carry much more weight than is appropriate.

Method Selection

Given these advantages and disadvantages, which data collection method is most appropriate for each stakeholder group or individual? You can use Worksheet 7.3 to make such choices. In the left column, list each stakeholder or group whose input you have decided to seek. In the right column, record which method would be best with each stakeholder.

3. INTERVIEW OR SURVEY STAKEHOLDERS TO DETERMINE DESIRED OUTCOMES

Now you're ready to contact stakeholders and learn what they expect and need from the process being redesigned. Here is information about how to proceed with whatever tool you have chosen.

Surveys

Dan Madison, a West Coast consultant with excellent re-engineering experience, uses the following questions when he surveys customers of a particular process:

1. What do you expect from this process?

2. What do you like about the process?

3. What don't you like about the process?

4. How would you rate the performance of the process?

   Excellent   Very Good   Average   Below Average   Failing

5. If you didn't rate it as excellent, how does it need to change to be excellent?

6. Do you know of any organization that does this process better?

You can ask stakeholders these six questions about the entire process. An alternative is to ask these questions about each *major phase* in the process, if it is a very large, complex process. For instance, one federal

WORKSHEET 7.3. Method Selection.

STAKEHOLDER GROUP	BEST DATA COLLECTION METHOD

government agency that redesigned its travel process asked these questions about the pretravel phase, and repeated them to learn about the posttravel phase.

Focus Groups

If you lead a focus group, you should follow the steps outlined here.

1. Decide the composition of the sample group you want to interview. Most focus groups have six to twelve members. Do you want the group to represent certain ages, ethnic backgrounds, genders, geographic areas, types of end users, and so forth?

2. Select your group. Tell them the reasons for the session and the ground rules (for example, how the information will be used, how confidential their comments will or will not be, and so on). Let them know whether they will get a copy of the focus group summary. To ensure uniformity, you can put this information in writing.

3. Plan all logistical details, arranging to have a comfortable place, a convenient time, refreshments, comfortable seats, a flip chart, and paper and pencils for the participants. Create and photocopy any handouts that you need. Well in advance of the meeting, mail the participants clear directions indicating the site, directions, time, and so forth.

4. Write the questions. Typically, you will have time for about five to seven questions in an hour-and-a-half session (two hours is probably as much as you can expect to get).

Use this guideline in designing the question sequence:

The questions should proceed from general to specific, from easy to difficult.

Start with general, easy questions. (For example, you could begin by asking, "When did you first have contact with our organization?") Let people warm into the session. Then, gradually become more specific, posing questions that may require participants to take time to reflect. ("When you think about the last few times you used our service, what exactly were you expecting from it? What did you get? If you didn't get what you expected, what accounts for the gap?")

Here are other tips on constructing good questions. Use openended questions, not those inviting "yes" or "no" responses. Use "how" and "what" types of questions. Prepare follow-up questions in advance for each question. (For instance, if someone says they never use a particular service, follow-up questions could include, "What makes this service not seem useful to you?" and "Have you ever used this service in the past?")

5. Put the questions in order. Focus groups should have three general phases:

Opening, purpose, introductions, and ground rules

Interview questions and discussion

Wrap-up

At the end, you could say: "I would like each of you to say one thing that you heard in this discussion that was really important to you."

6. Practice asking peers these questions. Role-play the interview, going through all the questions. At the end, ask your peers which questions were clear and which were confusing. Ask whether the sequence made sense. See if they interpreted each question as you intended. Make changes as needed.

7. Conduct the session. Have *at least* two staff members there, more if possible. One person should ask all of the questions; a second should be available to record responses, pick up on body language, and ask occasional follow-up questions as needed. Others may be there to act as experts on the process being discussed and to answer technical questions that the facilitator cannot answer.

8. Review the session within one to two days. Have all team members who were at the session go over their notes. Discuss both what was said in response to each question and how it was said (that is, discuss intensity of feeling, body language, and so on). Analyze the responses, looking for any common themes.

9. Write a report. List the questions and summarize the responses to each. Then conclude with a summary and overall analysis of the responses.

NOTE: For a sample focus group questionnaire and an actual example from one government design team, see Appendix A.

Individual Interviews

Once you've identified the people you want to interview individually, invite them to participate in the interview. Then, follow steps two through nine above. Consider conducting the session in the participant's office as a courtesy.

NOTE: Some teams quantify stakeholders' responses in a very precise manner. This may be appropriate, depending on the agency's culture. For instance, if you work with people who are very quantitatively oriented and who expect detailed analyses of each recommendation, you will benefit from quantifying stakeholder responses. The stakeholder gap analysis in Appendix B will help you do this.

4. COMPARE AND ANALYZE DATA FROM EACH STAKEHOLDER, SYNTHESIZING DESIRED OUTCOMES

Now that you've learned what the key stakeholders expect and need from the process, it's time to analyze the data and to determine which needs are most important to meet. When all key stakeholders want the same thing from a process, this step can be simple.

EXAMPLE:

A design team in Lynchburg, Virginia, was given the task of re-engineering the city's Capital Improvement Program (CIP) process. The CIP is the key process for planning and managing capital expenditures. It is a very important process for all local governments because of its impact on the community's growth and financial well-being.

The team learned that the stakeholders wanted this process to be

Flexible

Efficient

Inclusive (consensus driven)

Supported by the latest technology

Compliant with arbitrage regulations

After a series of focus groups and individual interviews, the design team determined the desired outcome for the process:

The CIP should be a simple process that funds and manages projects to meet the community's capital needs.

Once the team identified the process's desired outcome and key stakeholder needs, it was ready to move on and set stretch objectives for each need (described in Chapter Eight).

Often, however, stakeholders have different (even contradictory) needs and expectations. When this is the case, how can you determine the common expectations and needs?

1. Look for *recurring themes*. In some cases, most stakeholders will want the same thing. For instance, you may hear several stakeholders of the social service eligibility process say they want a process that is easy to understand.

2. Where stakeholders' needs and expectations differ, look for areas in which they have *underlying common interests*. Environmentalists often want the Environmental Protection Agency to have processes that scrutinize industrial practices very closely, whereas industry groups complain about micromanaging and want oversight processes that are unobtrusive. But both environmentalists and industry groups want oversight processes that are *predictable*. Look for examples of common interests. In the social services example, virtually all stakeholders want an eligibility process that is efficient and accurate.

Worksheet 7.4 asks you to go through a similar process of synthesizing stakeholder needs. By finding the common themes among them, you can determine the desired outcome of the process.

5. COMMUNICATE THE RESULTS TO KEY STAKEHOLDERS

NOTE: *Don't skip this step!* This is about ensuring effective implementation. It's never too early to build support for implementation!

I've seen some teams skip this step in their desire to get on with their project, but that's always a mistake. When people are interviewed or surveyed, they appreciate getting some feedback. This is especially important in the redesign of a process, because your stakeholders have, by definition, a key stake in your team's work. They are eager to know what you learned, what you make of what you learned, and how this information will affect the design of the new process. The sponsor should be involved in this communication process.

Furthermore, the cost of skipping this step is high. Many people today refuse to fill out surveys because their experience is that nobody gets back to them with the results. They think, "Nobody uses the information, so why should I bother to fill out the form? I don't need more 'feel-good' gestures from people who want to give the impression of listening to their customers. I want genuine listening and a response to my comments. Give me that, or don't ask me in the first place."

In short, communicating the results to key stakeholders helps to build their trust. It also adds to the credibility of the team's efforts. And it gives the team an opportunity to stay in touch with employees (a key stakeholder group) and build support for change. Employees don't need to know all of the details that the team learned from its surveys and focus groups, but they should hear the bottom line: which stakeholders were included, what their common needs and expectations were, and what outcome the redesigned process should achieve. You can communicate all this in writing or in person.

WORKSHEET 7.4. Summary of Stakeholders' Key Needs and Expectations.

1. What are the major stakeholder needs and expectations?

STAKEHOLDER	NEEDS AND EXPECTATIONS
_____	_____
_____	_____
_____	_____
_____	_____

2. What are the common themes?

3. What are the desired outcomes of this process, given the needs, expectations, and common themes?

6. DECIDE WHETHER YOU ARE READY TO MOVE ON TO THE NEXT DESIGN STEP

The purpose of "starting at the end" with stakeholder needs is to define the purpose of the process and the key needs and expectations it is to meet. You are ready to move on if your team can answer yes to the questions in Worksheet 7.5.

SUMMARY

The idea of "starting at the end" with the stakeholders' needs and the desired outcome is important at two levels. It gives you more data about the current process. Put the data together with what you learned from mapping the current process and you have a full picture of the process and its impact on key *people*—your end users and your employees.

This step also gives you important information about the *politics* of implementing your ultimate recommendations. As you learn more about your stakeholders' expectations and needs, you understand who is committed to the process as it now functions and who wants it changed. You find out more about the "pain" caused by the process and how that affects people. And you start to develop a constituency for change. There is no natural constituency for change, says Jack Welch of General Electric; you have to create it. By listening carefully to your stakeholders, getting back to them to summarize what you learned, and letting them know they are the reason you are redesigning the work, you are starting to build that constituency.

Now it's time to focus more specifically on the future. You need to take the desired outcomes you've identified and translate them into concrete goals. And those goals need to be so high that they force the design team to become innovative, to get out of the box. Such goals are called "stretch objectives." They are described in the next chapter.

WORKSHEET 7.5. Are You Ready to Move On?

1. Is there a clearly stated outcome for this process? _____

2. Do you understand the major stakeholder needs and expectations regarding this process? _____

3. Do you know the major gaps between what stakeholders need and what they currently feel they get from the process? _____

4. Have you communicated to your sponsor and key stakeholders what you learned during this step? _____

5. If you answered no to any of the above, what do you have to do to complete this phase?

_____

_____

_____

_____

_____

CHAPTER 8

Setting Your Stretch Objective

FIGURE 8.1. Four Steps for Redesigning a Process.

1. Map the current process

2. Establish the desired outcomes

3. Set a stretch objective

4. Design from a clean sheet

PURPOSE OF SETTING YOUR STRETCH OBJECTIVE

Stretch objectives reach far beyond what a process currently produces. A famous example is President Kennedy's 1961 challenge to "put a man on the moon and return him safely to Earth in this decade." Kennedy's statement did what all good stretch objectives do—it forced people to engage in out-of-the-box thinking and to accomplish what current processes and systems couldn't achieve.

The purpose of stretch objectives is to force staff members to abandon outmoded thinking about a process and to set one or more performance targets that they can only meet by using very innovative thinking and new ways of behaving.

OUTCOMES OF THIS STEP

Once the design team determines one or more stretch objectives, it will have a concrete target to shoot for in redesigning the current process. It will also be stimulated to come up with creative new designs for the process.

NOTE: For more on stretch objectives, see Linden, *Seamless Government*, 1994b, pp. 143–153.

EXAMPLES OF STRETCH OBJECTIVES

Stretch objectives are another name for *performance measures*. As such, they relate to the desired outcome of the process. They are usually (but not necessarily) stated in quantitative terms and should always be stated in a concrete way that is easily measured. As a guideline, stretch objectives should require performance improvements of 50 percent or more. Here are examples of possible stretch objectives from various agencies.

DESIRED OUTCOME	POSSIBLE STRETCH OBJECTIVES
Travelers will be reimbursed promptly.	Reimburse travelers within three days of submitting a voucher.
End users will be served with minimal waiting time.	Reduce waiting time by 80 percent.
Veterans will learn the status of their claims in a simple, user-friendly manner.	Veterans will not need to make more than one call to answer any question.

DESIRED OUTCOME *(CONTINUED)*	POSSIBLE STRETCH OBJECTIVES
Staff members will be able to purchase what they need, when they need it, with no hassles.	All small purchases will be received within five working days.
Program quality will improve, with a major reduction in costs.	End users' evaluation of programs will be 90 percent positive, and costs will go down by 65 percent.
Citizens will obtain permits through a process that applicants and staff members find easy to use.	People on both sides of the counter will be smiling.
America will have the world's premier space program.	We will put a man on the moon and return him safely to Earth in this decade.

NOTE: Performance measures are gaining in popularity among government and business leaders. This book can't do justice to such a large and complex topic. For one thoughtful treatment of performance measures, see Friedman, *A Guide to Developing and Using Performance Measures in Results-Based Budgeting,* 1997, available from the Finance Project, 1000 Vermont Ave. N.W., Washington, D.C. 20005.

Here are the substeps involved in creating stretch objectives:

1. Review stakeholders' needs and expectations.

2. Identify the needs and expectations that form the foundations of stretch objectives.

3. Brainstorm possible stretch objectives.

4. Decide whether you are ready to move on to the next design step.

1. REVIEW STAKEHOLDERS' NEEDS AND EXPECTATIONS

As you review the stakeholders' needs and expectations that you listed in Worksheet 7.4, which needs and expectations seem to be especially important to key stakeholders? These items may seem important for any or all of the following reasons:

They came up several times.

Stakeholders talked about them with intensity.

You could meet other critical needs if these needs were met.

They were noted by key stakeholders whose input is especially important to the organization.

2. IDENTIFY THE NEEDS AND EXPECTATIONS THAT FORM THE FOUNDATIONS OF STRETCH OBJECTIVES

It isn't necessary, or even helpful, to establish a large number of stretch objectives. Most design teams set from one to four, at most. Remember: stretch objectives should relate to the output of the second design step—the needs and expectations you're trying to meet—and to the process's overall purpose.

EXAMPLE:

In Chapter Seven, we discussed the Lynchburg, Virginia, design team that was given the project of re-engineering the city's capital improvement program process. The team learned that the major stakeholders needed the process to be

Flexible

Efficient

Inclusive (consensus driven)

Supported by the latest technology

Compliant with arbitrage regulations

The team then sets stretch objectives for each need.

NEED	STRETCH OBJECTIVE
Flexibility	90 percent of stakeholders rate the flexibility of the process as good or excellent.
Efficiency	90 percent of stakeholders rate the efficiency of the process as good or excellent.
	90 percent of the current year's project expenditures come within 10 percent of estimates.
Inclusiveness	90 percent of those project originators surveyed feel heard and considered.
	100 percent of submitted projects are reviewed and considered for adoption.
Technology	95 percent of status information on each capital project is available on-line.
Compliance	There is 100 percent compliance with arbitrage requirements.

There are several tried-and-true methods of determining the needs and expectations on which you want to base stretch objectives. The design team should ask itself the following questions:

Which stakeholder need or expectation, if exceeded, would lead to the satisfaction of several other needs and expectations?

EXAMPLE:

The U.S. Forest Service established a design team to redesign the special use permit process. The Forest Service issues such permits to build private cabins, campgrounds, marinas, and ski resorts and to use public lands for other private interests. The process has continually been criticized by various stakeholders, and Forest Service attorneys must frequently defend the agency against lawsuits relating to special use permits.

The steering team leading the project brainstormed several stretch objectives, debated them, and gave them to the design team. These stretch objectives related to cycle time, the staff hours required to process the permits, the use of a corporate database, staff members' technical competence, and customer satisfaction. The design team believed that the stretch objectives were not all of equal value. The first stretch objective was to cut by 50 percent the cycle time spent to process special use permits, as well as cutting the staff hours related to that work. The design team felt that attaining this objective would be the key to success; delivering on it would lead to accomplishing the others. The point here is to think strategically: which are the stretch objectives that are critical to achieving many positive outcomes?

Here's another question that the design team should consider:

Which needs are most important to stakeholders?

EXAMPLE:
The Prince William County team redesigning the rezoning process initially assumed that its stakeholders were most upset about the amount of time it took to complete the process. Its interviews and surveys, however, identified greater concerns: citizens found the application packet intimidating, they had no opportunity for face-to-face meetings with review agencies, and there was no opportunity for citizen involvement until late in the process. The team lumped these concerns together into one key stretch objective—boosting citizen satisfaction with the process from about 55 percent to 90 percent. The Prince William team understood a key point: we can't assume we know what customers want. We need to go out and listen to them.

Here's a third consideration:

Are certain stakeholders especially important to your organization's success?

EXAMPLE:
The Executive Leadership Council at the Veterans Affairs Medical Center in Erie, Pennsylvania, embarked on a huge re-engineering project to help the hospital deal with the emerging realities of diminishing budgets. They selected two key stretch objectives for the comprehensive care design team to achieve:

- Eliminate 75 percent of the handoffs in every clinical process

- Reduce by 50 percent the time physicians and other providers spend recording the results of exams and related clinical contacts

The leadership team believed that achieving these two huge objectives would free up staff to serve more patients, which would increase the hospital's revenue stream and put it in a stronger position vis-à-vis a very important stakeholder—the VA headquarters. They further reasoned that reduced waiting time would be important to their patients and that they would attract more business through word of mouth. Finally, reducing cycle time on exams and other paperwork is very important to physicians; many physicians who had left the VA cited paperwork requirements as a major reason for leaving.

Complete Worksheet 8.1 by listing the key stakeholder needs and expectations you want to target for stretch objectives. Then, next to each need listed, add information on the current performance of the process, that is, how well does it meet those needs?

3. BRAINSTORM POSSIBLE STRETCH OBJECTIVES FOR EACH NEED OR EXPECTATION

How do you come up with specific stretch objectives? They come from one perspective and from three potential sources.

A Helpful Perspective

Redesigning for seamless service is about meeting future needs and delivering future outcomes. It isn't rocket science, but it *is* hard work that requires time and resources. Don't waste your team's time trying to meet yesterday's or even today's end user needs. Those needs will change as your competition's performance improves, as technology improves, and as customer expectations increase. Focus on the future when you set stretch objectives.

Sources of Stretch Objectives

Stretch objectives can come from

1. Benchmarking the same processes performed by leading organizations

2. Customer and stakeholder requests and preferences

3. Your organization's best performance of the process

WORKSHEET 8.1. Bases for Stretch Objectives.

STAKEHOLDER NEEDS AND EXPECTATIONS	CURRENT PERFORMANCE DATA
1. _____	_____
2. _____	_____
3. _____	_____
4. _____	_____
5. _____	_____
6. _____	_____
7. _____	_____
8. _____	_____
9. _____	_____
10. _____	_____

Benchmarking

Benchmarking is a new term for an old idea—systematically learning from others. Some organizations use very complex methodologies for benchmarking today. For our purposes, a few simple steps work well:

- Identify a small number of organizations (four to seven) that perform the same process as yours.

- Visit or call managers who oversee the process in each organization, indicating that you are redesigning a process and want to learn about the performance of their process. (It usually helps to promise the organization a copy of your final report.)

- Record the key performance data about the organization's process, especially in the performance areas of greatest interest to your stakeholders (for example, time, cost, number of steps, how user friendly it is, quality, and so forth).

- Learn how the process is performed in that organization (not every step, but the basic approach). Are some things done very differently?

NOTE: For a more complete description of the benchmarking steps, see Appendix C.

EXAMPLE:
The Prince William County team redesigning its rezoning process obtained benchmark data from several local governments in Virginia, Maryland, and North Carolina. The results appear below.

SUMMARY OF BENCHMARKING STUDY (PRINCE WILLIAM COUNTY, VIRGINIA)

LOCALITY	PROCESSING TIME (MONTHS)	CASES/YEAR	REVIEW AGENCIES' PARTICIPATION	CITIZEN/COMMUNITY INVOLVEMENT BEFORE SUBMISSION
Howard Co., Md.	6–9	10	Written comments	None
James City Co., Wash.	4	50	Written comments	None
Henrico Co., Va.	2	70–90	Written comments	Some community meetings and informal review
Hickory, N.C.	1.5–2	10–15	Verbal comments	None
Arlington Co., Va.	3	7	Written or verbal comments	Applicant encouraged to meet with civic association before filing

Customer Preferences and Requests

Your team has already received considerable information from stakeholders. What did you learn about stakeholder ideas and preferences that might help you set a stretch objective?

Most customers keep a "report card" in their minds concerning service. When we receive especially good customer service, we often make a mental note of it. And we recall that service when another organization treats us poorly. Your design team may have heard customers and stakeholders make comments similar to the following:

> "Why can't I obtain this information on the Internet? Why do I have to come to your office?"

> "I like dealing with just one person when I purchase something. I don't appreciate having to deal with several different departments, especially when each is blissfully ignorant of what the others have been telling me."

> "Why do you send so many different people to my office? One day it's a building inspector, then it's a fellow from Public Service, then it'll be someone from the health department. Don't your people ever talk with each other? I was in the hospital last month, and everyone knew what others were doing. Why don't you?!"

These kinds of statements and questions are good sources of stretch objectives.

Your Organization's Best Performance

The third potential source of stretch objectives is your own best performance. What is the fastest you have ever performed this process? When did you have the fewest steps? The best quality? The biggest impact on customer satisfaction?

Of course you can cite an example, but it was an emergency, right? Or it was done on an exception basis, because the senior official required it immediately. Fine. The question then becomes, "What exactly did you do when you provided such excellent performance?" More important, "How could you do that routinely without killing the staff in the process?!"

HELPFUL HINT → **Consider a Stretch Objective That Involves Cycle Time** "Haste makes waste," right? Well, sometimes working faster does produce more mistakes. When something is done thoughtfully, however, faster usually leads to higher quality, not lower.

Since the mid 1980s, a great number of public and private organizations have learned that enormous amounts of time are wasted in their key work processes. This is time when no work goes on, when paper piles up, when forms wait for approvals, when things are done sequentially that could be done simultaneously, when a process is bogged down in paper.

I'm continually struck by how much time is wasted in most work processes. More important, I'm delighted by how quickly design teams find opportunities to reduce cycle time by 50 to 70 percent. I've seen teams reduce the time to hire new staff to less than four weeks (down from four to six months), provide city and county maps in five minutes (not five days), and send Social Security cards out in less than one week (down from forty days). There are dozens of other examples that show how well government agencies can deliver when they set high targets and determine to stop wasting time.

The old belief that haste makes waste is being turned on its head. Many teams learn that when they reduce cycle time by eliminating waiting time and non-value-adding steps, quality in fact goes up, not down. Why? Problems are spotted sooner. Unnecessary steps become more obvious and are eliminated. Focusing on time puts a premium on individual or team accountability, rather than spreading accountability over several different people. When people know they're accountable, they tend to be very particular about the quality.

Eliminating wasted time and steps makes for the "magic trio" of customer expectations these days: "Better, faster, cheaper."

Meet with Your Sponsor to Determine One or More Stretch Objectives

Establishing appropriate stretch objectives is a critical step when redesigning work processes. It's essential to obtain the input and agreement of your sponsor—and others, in some cases—before proceeding to redesign the process. When meeting with your sponsor to review your proposed stretch objectives, use Worksheet 8.2. The sponsor needs to agree with at least one stretch objective.

4. DECIDE WHETHER YOU ARE READY TO MOVE ON TO THE NEXT DESIGN STEP

The purpose of a stretch objective is to force staff to abandon outmoded work methods, think in innovative ways, and come up with a dramatically new design. You are ready to move on if your team can answer yes to each of the questions in Worksheet 8.3.

SUMMARY

This chapter focused on one of the keys to improving performance dramatically. Striving to achieve stretch objectives forces us to do what this workbook is all about—redesigning work to achieve seamless service. When we set a goal of 50 percent or greater improvement, we naturally start thinking in dramatically new ways.

WORKSHEET 8.2. Stretch Objectives Checklist.

1. What stretch objectives do we propose?

NEED	STRETCH OBJECTIVE	CURRENT PERFORMANCE ON THIS MEASURE (FOR EXAMPLE, CYCLE TIME, COST, CUSTOMER SATISFACTION)

(Worksheet 8.2 continued on next page)

2. How did we arrive at each stretch objective (benchmarking data, customer request, our own best performance, another source)?

PROPOSED STRETCH OBJECTIVE	ARRIVED AT THROUGH BENCHMARKING	ARRIVED AT THROUGH CUSTOMER REQUESTS	ARRIVED AT THROUGH OUR OWN BEST PERFORMANCE
_____	_____	_____	_____
_____	_____	_____	_____
_____	_____	_____	_____
_____	_____	_____	_____
_____	_____	_____	_____
_____	_____	_____	_____
_____	_____	_____	_____
_____	_____	_____	_____
_____	_____	_____	_____

3. What does the sponsor say about these objectives?

STRETCH OBJECTIVE	SPONSOR INPUT

4. With which stretch objectives does the sponsor agree?

_____

_____

_____

_____

WORKSHEET 8.3. Are You Ready to Move On?

1. Have you identified the most important needs and expectations that this process should meet? _____

2. Have you benchmarked the performance of leading organizations that have the same process? _____

3. Have you considered key stakeholders' requests and desires in terms of the performance they want this process to achieve? _____

4. Have you looked at the very best your own organization has achieved in performing this process? _____

5. Have you reviewed your proposed stretch objectives with your sponsor and found that the sponsor agrees with one or more stretch objectives? _____

6. If you answered no to any of the above, what do you have to do to complete this phase?

_____

_____

_____

_____

_____

Thus, setting stretch objectives helps to overcome some of the *political* barriers to redesigning work, because it gives everyone involved a common challenge. The support of the project sponsor and steering team sends a signal to others that this goal is real and that the design team must do whatever it takes to achieve it. Members of the design team, and to a lesser extent the project sponsor and the steering team, are the key *people* involved in setting stretch objectives. Some steering teams like to take the lead in setting these objectives, and there are times when that's appropriate, but in general it's best done by the design team with steering team agreement.

In terms of the overall redesign *plan,* setting stretch objectives focuses the project clearly on the future. Up to this point, the design team has analyzed the present (how the process currently works, what stakeholders want from the process) and has made some guesses about the future (how stakeholder needs might change). Setting stretch objectives has pointed the design team toward the future. That future starts with a clean sheet on which the design team can paint a radically new picture. We will explore that in the next chapter.

CHAPTER 9

Designing from a Clean Sheet

FIGURE 9.1. Four Steps for Redesigning a Process.

1. Map the current process
2. Establish the desired outcomes
3. Set a stretch objective
4. Design from a clean sheet

PURPOSE OF DESIGNING FROM A CLEAN SHEET

The purpose of designing the new process from a clean sheet is to help the team come up with ideas that lead to a dramatically improved process. It's difficult if not impossible to make a fundamental change if we start with our current process firmly fixed in our minds and ask ourselves how to improve it. Beginning with a clean sheet challenges us to turn our backs on the map of the current process and to ask this question:

If we could start over, with no history or turf problems, and if our only task were to achieve the process's desired outcomes and meet our stretch objectives, how would we do it?

OUTCOMES OF THIS STEP

When the team finishes designing from a clean sheet, it will have a new process that key stakeholders have reviewed and that the team can present to the steering team.

HOW TO BEGIN DESIGNING FROM A CLEAN SHEET

Here are the substeps involved.

1. Post stakeholder needs and stretch objectives on the wall to summarize progress.

2. Review design principles.

3. Review the assumptions on which your current process is based.

4. Brainstorm ideas for the new process. List common themes among the ideas.

5. Create flow charts reflecting new processes. Test the new designs.

6. Obtain feedback from the sponsor and key stakeholders.

7. Choose a design. Refine the map of the new process.

8. Determine what policy and organizational changes the process will require.

9. Decide whether you are ready to move on to the next phase.

1. POST STAKEHOLDER NEEDS AND STRETCH OBJECTIVES ON THE WALL TO SUMMARIZE PROGRESS

Put sheets on the wall that show the desired outcomes for this process and the stretch objectives the team needs to meet. This step may seem unnecessary, but it's very useful. For both symbolic and substantive reasons, having the outcomes and stretch objectives visibly posted will help the team come up with a clean sheet design. Every time an idea is considered, it should be tested against the desired outcomes and objectives.

2. REVIEW DESIGN PRINCIPLES

Teams find it helpful to discuss design principles when they begin with a clean sheet. Here is a short list of such principles. Teams should consider additional design principles from their own experience.

- Organize around outcomes, not functions and departments.

- Bring downstream information upstream. The needs and information of those who deal with the process in later stages ("downstream") must be made available to those who work "upstream" at the start of the process. That's where it can have the greatest impact.

- Capture information once, at the source, and share it widely. Every time information is entered, it creates a possibility of error, delay, turf building, and frustration for staff and customers.

- Provide a single contact point for customers and suppliers. The more employees a customer must deal with to obtain a service or product, the less satisfaction customers have with the organization. Replace fragmented processes with simple, integrated ones, and give one person the responsibility of answering all questions about these processes.

- Substitute parallel for sequential processes. Doing work one step at a time may have made sense in the low-tech, industrial era; it makes no sense in a high-tech, speed-oriented era. To respond quickly to changing demands and to integrate the work of various work units, have them perform the work simultaneously.

- Maintain a continuous flow of the "main sequence" (those steps that add value to the end user):

    Identify and eliminate non-value-adding steps.
    Use triage, not a one-size-fits-all strategy.

- Don't pave cow paths. First, redesign the process. Then, support it with technology.

NOTE: These principles are described in detail, with numerous public and private sector examples, in Chapter Four of Linden, *Seamless Government*, 1994b.

3. REVIEW THE ASSUMPTIONS ON WHICH YOUR CURRENT PROCESS IS BASED

In Worksheet 6.8, you listed the assumptions that underlie your current process. Which are still valid and should be retained in the new process? Which are no longer valid and should be replaced by different assumptions?

Many organizational processes assume that most employees are likely to cheat. For instance, the time and attendance process in most public (and private) bureaucracies sends a message that employees are likely to cheat if their actual work time is not carefully monitored. This assumption is being challenged in many progressive organizations today that have switched to a management-by-exception approach whereby employees are assumed to be working their normal hours unless there is evidence to the contrary.

In some state and local governments, and at federal agencies such as the General Accounting Office, the payroll system automatically pays the employee the regular pay every payday unless information about overtime or leave is provided. This system saves time; employees don't fill out leave sheets, supervisors don't have to sign them, secretaries don't run around trying to find managers to approve them, and payroll clerks don't have to total the numbers every two or four weeks for most employees. It tells employees that they are trusted to do the right thing. That's the new assumption—that most employees don't cheat.

Ah, but what about those who do cheat? Some will. But think about it—some cheat using the current system! Furthermore, under the management-by-exception system, the organization makes a positive statement to employees, rather than a controlling, distrustful one. Chances are, more employees will cheat in a negative, control-oriented system than in a positive one. And think about all the time you've saved. . . .

4. BRAINSTORM IDEAS FOR THE NEW PROCESS, LIST COMMON THEMES AMONG THE IDEAS

SPEED BUMP

The Design Team Has Trouble Getting Out of the Box Some design teams find it hard to develop truly innovative ideas. They're too used to hearing people utter "killer phrases," statements that immediately take the wind out of their sails. Killer phrases include such delightful comments as

"It's not in the budget."

"Senior management won't buy it."

"We've never done it that way."

"We've always done it this way."

"You've got to be kidding!"

The design team needs to take some specific actions to free itself from such limitations so that it can come up with innovative solutions.

NOTE: For more on killer phrases and how to diffuse them, see Appendix D.

 HELPFUL HINTS

Warm Up! Get Out of the Usual Meeting Room. Try Groupware.

1. Before you start brainstorming, exercise your creative juices. Check out the creativity exercises in Appendix D or use others that team members like. You're going into a new mode now. You need to let go of your careful, logical, left-brain style and allow yourselves to become silly and courageous. Don't jump in immediately. Warm into it.

2. When your team starts brainstorming, go somewhere else. It could be another room in the building, a meeting room in a hotel or restaurant, or the home of one of your team members. More important than where you go is the idea of changing your setting. All you need is your list of stakeholder needs, the desired outcome, and your stretch objectives. Those, and some clean sheets on the wall.

3. If you have access to it, look for a room equipped with a wonderful technology called groupware, the kind that supports electronic (and anonymous) brainstorming. Groupware-equipped rooms have a set of laptops for teams to use. There is a large screen in front of the room. When the team leader or facilitator poses a question (for example, "What are some of our initial ideas for improving this process?"), everyone types in responses. The responses appear on the large screen in random order, with no names attached. The benefits are impressive:

- Everyone is immediately involved, ensuring real productivity.
- All ideas are anonymous, ensuring honesty.
- Everyone works simultaneously, ensuring that a few strong voices don't drown out the rest.
- You can respond to someone else's idea on the large screen, ensuring interaction.
- The group can generate fifty or more ideas in a matter of minutes, ensuring efficiency. Group members electronically discuss the ideas. Then they sort them, rank them (assigning weight to different categories), and vote. Using groupware, I have seen teams do in two hours what would otherwise take several days to a week.

 HELPFUL HINT

Remember the Key Guidelines for Brainstorming

- Go for quantity at first; don't worry about quality.

- No criticism is allowed.

- "Piggyback" on others' ideas.

You can use Worksheet 9.1 to record the team's ideas. Write them down in any order.

Keep this in mind during brainstorming:

Most great ideas were initially ridiculed.

I must confess that my imagination . . . refuses to see any sort of submarine doing anything but suffocating its crew and floundering at sea.

—H. G. Wells, British novelist, 1901

There is no reason anyone would want a computer in their home.

—Ken Olson, chairman and founder, Digital Equipment Corporation, 1977

Group the ideas in Worksheet 9.1 with similar themes.

1. If there are several ideas about reducing the number of handoffs and approvals, these might suggest that one person or a self-directed work team should do the entire process from start to finish.

2. If there are several ideas about multiple forms and about how the same data is entered several times, these might suggest a new process that incorporates advanced technology creatively.

5. CREATE FLOW CHARTS REFLECTING NEW PROCESSES, TEST THE NEW DESIGNS

Do you recall the example of the old grading permits process, which was shown in Worksheet 6.5? Well, the design team conceived a new process, which is depicted in Worksheet 9.2 as a high-level flow chart.

Triage replaces one-size-fits-all in the new process, and generalists replace specialists to review 75 percent of the applications. The results have been dramatic: radically reduced cycle times, no loss in quality of review, much higher customer satisfaction, and significantly improved employee morale.

Once you have looked for common themes among your teams' ideas, develop at least two different concepts for the new process and sketch a simple flow chart depicting each. Use Worksheet 9.3 to draw these.

Now that you have two or more concepts and high-level maps for a new process design, it's time to test them out. The criteria rating forms

WORKSHEET 9.1. List of Team Ideas.

IDEAS	THEMES
1. _____	1. _____
2. _____	2. _____
3. _____	3. _____
4. _____	4. _____
5. _____	5. _____
6. _____	6. _____
7. _____	7. _____
8. _____	8. _____
9. _____	9. _____
10. _____	10. _____
11. _____	
12. _____	
13. _____	
14. _____	
15. _____	
16. _____	
17. _____	
18. _____	
19. _____	
20. _____	

WORKSHEET 9.2. Sample High-Level Flow Chart.

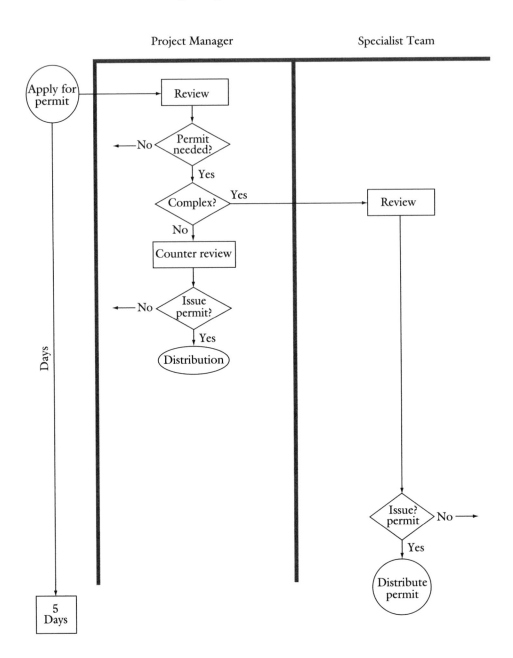

WORKSHEET 9.3. Your High-Level Flow Chart.

Design 1:

Design 2:

shown in Worksheets 9.4 and 9.5 can help you compare the current process with your proposed process designs. With such a form, you can determine whether the to-be process meets the end user's needs, the desired outcome for the process, and the stretch objective. You can also see whether your proposed process matches the performance of leading organizations. Using Worksheet 9.4 as a model, fill in Worksheet 9.5 for each of the new process designs you are considering.

Here's how to use the form:

1. List the categories of customer needs and expectations in the first column of the form (for example, speed, convenience, durability, and so forth).

2. In the second column, indicate measures of these specific customer needs and expectations (for instance, customers may define "Speed" as "Responds to request within twenty minutes").

3. In the third column, note the importance (high, medium, or low) that customers place on each need.

4. Enter the performance data for the current process in the "as-is process" column (for example, a forty-five minute response time).

5. In the fifth column, show the performance of your benchmark partners (for example, a twenty-five minute response time).

6. In the next-to-last column, indicate the stretch objective (perhaps a fifteen minute response time).

7. In the last column, show the expected performance of the to-be process (a fifteen minute response time).

The criteria rating form is a powerful tool to use when you write up the business case for the proposed process (see Chapter Ten).

6. OBTAIN FEEDBACK FROM THE SPONSOR AND KEY STAKEHOLDERS

Ask the sponsor whether some of the team's ideas shouldn't be shared yet with stakeholders. It may make sense not to share some ideas if

They are too politically sensitive.

The steering team would never accept them and would resent having stakeholders' expectations raised unnecessarily.

They are simply too expensive at this time.

WORKSHEET 9.4. Sample Criteria Rating Form: Department of Motor Vehicles.

CUSTOMER NEEDS AND EXPECTATIONS			CURRENT PERFORMANCE		FUTURE PERFORMANCE	
Criterion	Measure	Importance to Customer (H, M, L)	As-Is Process	Benchmark Partner's Process	Stretch Objective	Expected Performance
Speed	Process completed in less than 20 minutes	H	45 minutes	25 minutes	15 minutes	15 minutes
Convenience	Office open evenings and weekends	M	M–F, 8:00–4:30	Open 1 evening and Saturday morning	Open 4 evenings and all day Saturday	Open evenings and Saturday
Attractive license photo	Customer pleased with photo	H	30 percent satisfied	50 percent satisfied	75 percent satisfied	100 percent satisfied; customers will choose from several photos

WORKSHEET 9.5. Your Criteria Rating Form.

CUSTOMER NEEDS AND EXPECTATIONS			CURRENT PERFORMANCE		FUTURE PERFORMANCE	
Criterion	Measure	Importance to Customer (H, M, L)	As-Is Process	Benchmark Partner's Process	Stretch Objective	Expected Performance

They are difficult to summarize simply, and it wouldn't be in the team's interest to put out short sound bites that would likely be misinterpreted and create antagonism.

These and other reasons may argue against sharing certain ideas with your key stakeholders. However, my experience over and over is that the default should be toward openness with stakeholder groups. Once a team has discussed an idea and it seems to be a keeper, it should be shared unless a powerful argument can be made to keep it within the family. The team will build goodwill and confidence as it demonstrates its openness. It will also hear useful reactions and critiques at a time when it can still use those reactions to improve its ideas. You can record stakeholders' responses in Worksheet 9.6.

Why spend so much time listening to stakeholders? Because there is no natural constituency for change. You must create one! And involving stakeholders is an excellent way to create such a constituency.

One way to create that constituency is by informing and involving stakeholders. Some projects become very controversial inside the organization. When an external group becomes an advocate for the proposed change, however, it's much harder for employees to block the change and protect their turf. Public sector officials have successfully developed a broader, external constituency for change in the following situations:

- When the president goes "over the head of Congress" and appeals directly to the American people to support one of the administration's initiatives, he is trying to create a broader constituency for change.

- When the Oregon governor and state legislature involved thousands of citizens in developing a series of benchmarks (for example, reducing teenage pregnancy by a certain percentage, improving kids' reading scores by another percentage, and so on), and committed state agencies to work with each other and with local officials to meet these targets by certain dates, they were creating a broad constituency for change.

The sponsor must work closely with the steering team when trying to create a constituency for change, given the steering team's broader responsibilities.

WORKSHEET 9.6. Stakeholder Reactions to the Design.

STAKEHOLDER	REACTIONS TO DESIGN	OTHER COMMENTS
1. _____	_____	_____
_____	_____	_____
2. _____	_____	_____
_____	_____	_____
3. _____	_____	_____
_____	_____	_____
4. _____	_____	_____
_____	_____	_____
5. _____	_____	_____
_____	_____	_____

7. CHOOSE A DESIGN, REFINE THE MAP OF THE NEW PROCESS

Once you have reactions and suggestions from each stakeholder and your sponsor, it's time to make a decision about the best design to use. Use Worksheet 9.7.

After you have selected the best design for your new process, you can refine the flow chart you created in Worksheet 9.3. Your changes will reflect any of the feedback you received from stakeholders and from your sponsor. Use the space in Worksheet 9.8 to draw a new version of the flow chart.

HELPFUL HINT

Run a Quick Pilot or Simulation of the To-Be Process Conducting a simulation of the process can accomplish several goals. First, it will reveal unintended consequences of the process. It will also help the design team develop a realistic understanding of the new process. Furthermore, a simulation is an opportunity to involve key stakeholders, such as human resources and information technology staff. Simulations and pilots also provide opportunities to involve skeptics and to test out their concerns. Simulations can be run in real time or on the computer. There are several good simulation programs available today. Look at a publication such as *PCWeek* or *InfoWorld* for reviews of these products.

8. DETERMINE WHAT POLICY AND ORGANIZATIONAL CHANGES THE PROCESS WILL REQUIRE

Designing a new process involves more than the flow of steps. The design team now has to move back from the lofty heights of high conceptual designs and turn to practical considerations of policies and resources. Policies may need to be changed to eliminate certain approvals, checks, and handoffs. There may be a need to change certain job descriptions or reporting relationships to support the new process. In Worksheet 9.9, you should identify the changes needed to support the new process design.

What policies may have to change to support the new design? What about changes in organizational structure or reporting relationships? Will people need to be trained for new roles and skills? What about costs? There will be implementation costs (training, possibly new information systems, and so on). And the steering team will want to know whether the ongoing costs of running the new process will be higher or lower than current costs. The design team will enhance its chances for success by considering these questions now. If the steering team asks such questions and the design team isn't prepared, credibility goes south!!

WORKSHEET 9.7. Design Selection.

DESIGN NUMBER	ADVANTAGES	DISADVANTAGES	OTHER CONSIDERATIONS

What process design (or combination of designs) best meets stakeholder needs and expectations and achieves our desired outcomes and stretch objectives?

WORKSHEET 9.8. Your New High-Level Flow Chart.

WORKSHEET 9.9. An Estimate of Policy and Organizational Changes Needed.

Policy changes: _____

_____

_____

_____

_____

Organizational changes: _____

_____

_____

_____

_____

Roles and job description changes: _____

_____

_____

_____

_____

Anticipated costs of implementing and managing the new process: _____

_____

_____

_____

_____

EXAMPLE:

A team from the U.S. Department of Agriculture redesigned its travel process. The new design was based on a philosophy of pushing authority and responsibility for managing travel to the program offices (as opposed to having it all rest on the travel office). With the new process, there were far fewer approvals involved. The philosophy and stretch objectives required major changes in policy (the number of approvals required) and in roles and responsibilities (there was now greater authority and responsibility at the program office level).

HELPFUL HINTS

1. Involve technical experts who aren't on the design team in estimating the costs and policy and organizational implications of the new process.

2. Use this step as an opportunity to involve more people. Doing so will help in two ways. First, it creates that larger constituency noted above. Second, it can increase your credibility if people who are not on the team look at your design, support it, and contribute to your report.

9. DECIDE WHETHER YOU ARE READY TO MOVE ON TO THE NEXT PHASE

The purpose of beginning with a clean sheet is to come up with out-of-the-box ideas that help the team craft a dramatically improved process. You are ready to move on to the next step if you can answer yes to the questions in Worksheet 9.10.

SUMMARY

This chapter focused on the most exciting part of redesigning for seamless service—coming up with a creative blueprint for the to-be process. It's exhilarating work; it can also be a difficult time for the design team because those who are more practical and pragmatic will have a hard time suppressing their "Yes, but . . ." responses to some of the radical ideas that the more innovative members put forth. Design teams need to be patient with each other at this point. They also need to remain very focused on the desired outcomes and stretch objectives.

Following the steps outlined in this chapter gives the design team excellent exposure to key *people* in the redesign process. Technical experts, customers, and other stakeholders will be reviewing the team's ideas and adding their own. This involvement, of course, helps build the *political* case for change. And the team emerges from this step with the core of its final *plan*—the design for the proposed process.

This core needs to be surrounded by the rationale for change. This rationale or business case would explain what the current process involves and why it's inadequate, would document the team's steps, and would include information gleaned from benchmark partners. This final report must be at once accurate and persuasive. The next chapter will tell you how to create just such a business case.

WORKSHEET 9.10. Are You Ready to Move On?

1. Did you brainstorm ideas to meet the stakeholders' needs and the stretch objectives? _____

2. Have you developed two or more concepts and high-level flow charts for the new process? _____

3. Did you test each new process design against the desired outcomes, stakeholder needs, and stretch objectives? _____

4. Have you included your sponsor and some key stakeholders in reviewing each process design? _____

5. Have you chosen a design? _____

6. Have you identified the necessary policy and organizational changes and the likely implementation costs? _____

7. If you answered no to any of the above, what must you do to move to the next step?

_____

_____

_____

_____

Ensuring Successful Implementatiom

CHAPTER 10

Writing and Making Your Business Case

The design team's final report is sometimes called the business case. It sets forth the as-is process that the team analyzed, and it offers a solution—the to-be process.

PURPOSE OF WRITING A BUSINESS CASE

The purpose of writing a business case is to give the steering team a thorough understanding of the *w*'s and *h*'s of your work—the what, why, when, where, who, and how of redesigning this process. In addition, a well-written and well-documented business case is a marketing tool; it demonstrates the amount of homework and analysis the design team has done, it gives the steering team greater confidence in the design team's methodology, and it therefore increases the chances that the steering team will accept the final recommendations.

OUTCOMES OF THE STEP

After the design team has written the business case, it should have a well-researched proposal, a confident steering team, and a to-be process that is ready for implementation.

KEY ROLE OF THE SPONSOR

The team's sponsor must remain closely involved with the team throughout, especially at this point. *There can be absolutely no surprises between the sponsor and the design and steering teams.* As the design team moves toward completing its work and prepares to make recommendations, the sponsor should become increasingly involved in determining what to emphasize in the report.

The sponsor should help the design team research the way in which the steering team likes to receive information. Does it want a short, succinct report or a highly detailed one? Does it want to be briefed on the highlights before receiving the written report? The sponsor should let the design team know of any particular concerns that the steering team will express, so that those concerns can be clearly addressed in the report. And the sponsor should help the design team prepare to present the report. It may help to do a dry run, in which one or more design team members present the report and the sponsor plays the part of the steering team, asking the kinds of questions that steering team members are likely to ask.

STEPS IN WRITING A BUSINESS CASE

1. The design team should meet with the sponsor and discuss the following:

- Specific concerns that the steering team might have with the recommendations

- Ways in which the design team might deal with these concerns

- The level of detail or generality that the steering team prefers

- The kinds of presentations or reports that have been especially effective in the past with the steering team

2. Using the information from the sponsor, the design team should write a draft of the report. There are many possible formats; here is one I've found helpful:

- Executive summary that includes all the key information listed below:

    Reason for the project
    Names of the design and steering teams' members
    Name of the sponsor

Key problems found with the current process
Key changes recommended for the to-be process
Overall to-be philosophy or vision for the new process
Policy and organizational implications of implementing the project
Anticipated benefits and costs

- Team charter

- Names of key people involved:

  Design team members
  Nonmembers who were contacted during the project, including customers, staff, stakeholders, steering team members, subject matter experts, organizations benchmarked, and so forth

- Methodology used by team (that is, the four design steps)

- Analysis of the current process (flow chart, cycle time, costs and benefits, staff and customer frustrations, and underlying assumptions)

- Stakeholder needs, expectations, and desired outcomes for the process (what stakeholders like and don't like about the as-is process, what current and future needs the process must meet, and data from stakeholder surveys and focus groups)

- Benchmarking results

- Stretch objectives set by the design team, sponsor, and steering team

- To-be proposal (overall philosophy or vision of the new process, design of the new process, flow chart of the steps)

- Anticipated benefits of the to-be process for stakeholders, staff, and the organization

- Anticipated costs of the to-be process (especially in terms of implementation), such as new technology requirements, training requirements, and ongoing management of the new process

- Organizational implications of the to-be process, including changes in policies, training, information technology, role description, and reporting relationships

- The to-be process's contribution to the organization's overall direction, including strategic objectives that the new process supports, current change initiatives to which it relates, and its consistency with those other initiatives

- Implementation strategy, including possible makeup of implementation team, anticipated timeline with expected milestones along the way, and suggestions about pilots of the whole or partial to-be process

- Communications strategy, including the people who should be responsible for communications during implementation and the way employees can be informed and updated about the new process's purpose and the status of implementation

3. When the draft is complete, the design teams should ask the sponsor to critique it. If the sponsor thinks it useful, the design team should share the draft with the steering team's leader.

4. The design team should use the feedback from step 3 to revise and finish the business case.

5. The design team should present the business case to the steering team.

 The design team can hit several speedbumps while writing and presenting the business case.

- Lack of proper communication with the rest of the organization can be a problem at this point. Rumors can start quickly if the design team doesn't ensure that the key ideas of the to-be model are communicated to other employees.

- The design team will be so familiar with its to-be model at this point that it might assume that the steering team is also familiar with the project's full details and remembers everything that the design team has communicated about the project.

- When presenting the business case to the steering team, some design teams fall into the understandable trap of trying to make the presentation a team effort. I've seen design teams include all six or eight members in presenting their final report. The result is usually a low-quality effort. Does that mean that one person should take, prepare, and present the final report? Not at all—there are many roles to play at this important stage. However, it usually does mean that only one or two should give the actual presentation, with the rest of the team there to answer questions if needed.

 When preparing the business case, the design team should keep a few pointers in mind.

- Although the design team may have done an excellent job of keeping key stakeholders informed of its efforts, nobody else understands its work as thoroughly as the design team does. Thus, the KISS (Keep It Simple, Stupid!) rule applies in writing the business case.

- Include graphics to portray major points: flow charts of as-is and to-be processes, charts showing data collected from stakeholders (such as the criteria rating form), and so forth.

Another effective use of graphics is to display the as-is process map next to the to-be map. Usually, there is a dramatic difference in terms of the number of steps and the obvious new simplicity. Figure 10.1 shows a good example from the Erie, Pennsylvania, Veterans Affairs Medical Center, which is redesigning many of its work processes. These maps depict the old and new preoperative education processes.

- Include the philosophy or vision for the new process. For instance, the Department of Defense Task Force to Re-Engineer Travel issued the following statement:

[We will] manage travel as mission support, not as an end in itself. Treat the traveler and commander as responsible professionals and as honest customers of the travel system, not as presumed incompetents or criminals, and treat the commander as a responsible manager.

- List options for change that were considered but rejected, including the reasons they were rejected. This gives the team's final recommendation more credibility. It demonstrates that the design team didn't simply "buy the first car it saw on the lot"; instead, it did a good deal of homework and can back up its final recommendation.

- An alternative to recommending one design and showing why other options were rejected is to offer senior managers several options, listing the advantages and disadvantages of each. That's exactly what a team from Lynchburg, Virginia, did when it redesigned the city's travel process. The team recommended using a city credit card for most travel expenses (seminar registrations, meals and lodging, and so forth) and reimbursing employees from petty cash for out-of-pocket expenses during one-day trips. But during the presentation, the team listed the advantages and disadvantages of the three options it considered and compared those options to the city's current system (see Figure 10.2).

- Make it easy for the steering team to say yes by focusing the presentation on the big ideas and on senior managers' interests and concerns.

- Discuss the anticipated impact that the proposed process will have on other change projects or ongoing processes. Offer ideas for integrating the changes and communicating the results to all employees.

- Help the steering team start to think about implementation. The steering team will appreciate any suggestions that make life easier for senior managers. One of many ways the design team can do that is to offer concrete guidance on implementing the new process. You will find many ways to offer such guidance in Chapter Twelve.

It isn't the design team's job to write a complete implementation plan. However, if it gives specific implementation ideas to the steering team, the chances of having the proposal approved will increase. By supplying such suggestions, the design team is in effect saying to senior management, "We know that your job isn't easy, and we want to share some of the responsibility with you to see that our work becomes a reality."

FIGURE 10.1. Preoperative Education Process.

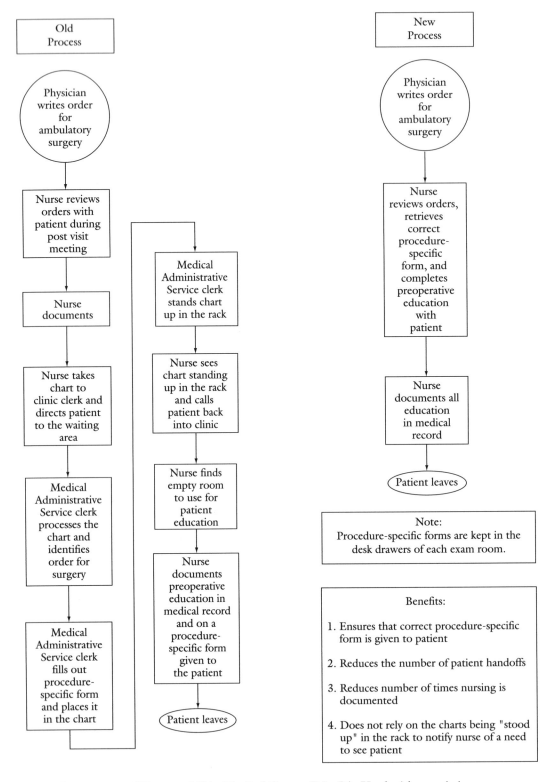

Source: Department of Veterans Affairs Medical Center, Erie, PA. Used with permission.

FIGURE 10.2. Three Alternatives to the Current Travel Process: Lynchburg, VA.

Desired Outcomes	Current System		Current System and Petty Cash		Current System and Per Diem		Credit Card and Petty Cash	
	Pro	Con	Pro	Con	Pro	Con	Pro	Con
Simplicity (no hassle)	No meal receipts required	Paper intensive; Requires director's signature	Small money immediate	More cash exposure + current system cons; Petty cash reconciliation for custodian	Eliminates some reconciliation	Current system cons	Small, large, and limited money exposure; Less paper; No manual checks; No voided checks due to canceled trips	Controls misuse; Have to bring all receipts; Have to log out credit card
Speed in receiving money		2 to 6 weeks turnaround	Small money immediate	Large money; Same turnaround; Petty cash custodian		2 to 6 weeks turnaround	Immediate availability of large and small money	
Convenience		Emergency money not easily available; Paperwork and turnaround time	Small money convenient in department	Emergency large money unavailable; Paperwork and turn-around time	No reconciliation for meals	Emergency money not available; Turnaround time; Cash not readily available	Immediately (24 hours); Accepted universally; Time savings	Difficult to find machine when out of town
Authority signatures?	Internal control	2 steps or more; Signer doesn't know what it is; Signer may not be in same office or building	Cash for day trip readily available; Emergency trips covered	Petty cash custodian will be involved; more responsibility	Internal control	2 steps or more; Signer doesn't know what it is; Signer may not be in same office or building	Department authority at division level	Petty cash custodian involved; more responsibility

Continued on next page

FIGURE 10.2. Three Alternatives to the Current Travel Process: Lynchburg, VA. (*Continued*)

Desired Outcomes	Current System		Current System and Petty Cash		Current System and Per Diem		Credit Card and Petty Cash	
	Pro	Con	Pro	Con	Pro	Con	Pro	Con
Accountability							Relieves finance of approval responsibility; In line with future direction of city — "ownership" of process	
City benefits	"We've always done it this way"	Cost of reservation check			Save cost of cutting recon. check; Limit cost of meals	May tempt honest employee to be dishonest	No check for hotel reservations (room deposit)	
Employee pro and con		Ties up employee credit			Employee accountable for funds received from city for per diem unused/etc. ("Trust Issue")		Immediate receipt of $ spent; Will not have to use personal credit card for lodging reservations	
Paperless process (reduce paper) integrated technology			Key at department level		Key at dept. level; One check instead of multiple		Key at dept. level One check instead of multiple; Quicker turnaround Save city $	
Consistency among departments		None		None	Possible		Possible	

SUMMARY

The ideas in this chapter about writing a business case all apply to your *plan*. However, in many ways these ideas are more targeted to one set of key *people*—the steering team—and to the *politics* of implementation. When you follow the steps outlined above, you show your awareness of and sensitivity to the world of senior managers. You give them a "security blanket"—namely, the information they need in an easily understood format. You are also giving them the assurance they require that the key people who could scuttle your idea have been involved from the start. In other words, you are practicing the fine art of "managing upward," an art that is frequently overlooked by otherwise very bright people. You are making it easier for a group who may be prone to saying no, or "We'll consider it," to give you a strong yes.

CHAPTER 11

Communicating and Marketing Your Project

We've emphasized the importance of having ongoing communications during the project. In Chapter Two, we discussed *who* should lead a communication effort and *what* that person or group should communicate. This chapter describes the *how* of communications.

SELLING THE VISION

Change requires marketing. Good works don't necessarily sell themselves.

When a creative engineer at 3M came up with the concept of Post-it® Notes, none of the 3M executives were taken with it. 3M had always made products that stuck together; Post-it® Notes were different because they didn't stick, at least not for long. The engineer sent Post-it® samples to the secretaries of the 3M executives; the secretaries started using them, loved them, and asked their bosses for more. That got the bosses' attention, and soon they began learning more about this strange new prototype. The rest, as they say, is history.

The lesson is clear. The facts don't necessarily speak for themselves. A vision becomes reality because some people work hard to sell the vision.

DRIVING THE POINT HOME

You never see a commercial just once.

Repetition is a key to effective communication. The words don't have to be precisely the same each time (some variation can help), but the essence of the message must be consistent and must be reinforced by senior executives' behavior. For instance, if the redesign effort is the organization's top priority this year, staff must see senior management actively spending time on the project. And the change leaders must be prepared to discuss the main message over and over in interactive sessions with staff units. When the first year of his change effort had ended, one government executive put it this way: "After I gave my change talk fifty times, I was sick and tired of uttering the words. But it was only then that the message started to get through."

COMMUNICATING EFFECTIVELY

There is a hierarchy of communication effectiveness.

More Effective

Involving people

Having small group, face-to-face discussions

Listening and seeing

Listening

Less Effective

Listening

Listening is the most passive activity. Relying solely on speeches, memos, and newsletters is not terribly useful.

Listening and Seeing

As we noted in the last chapter, using graphics helps. Show employees a picture of where the organization is today and how the change project will make it better tomorrow. Send the as-is and to-be maps around the organization. You can show the project milestones on a timeline. The Lynchburg, Virginia, design team that redesigned the organization's travel process (as noted in Chapter Ten) made creative use of graphics. They used Figure 11.1 to depict the current process as an impossible maze, and then they presented Figure 11.2 to show how the new process bypasses the maze.

Having Small-Group, Face-to-Face Discussions

Having small-group, face-to-face discussions is the most time-consuming communication activity; it's also one of the most effective. The importance of face-to-face meetings was reinforced by a survey conducted in Wake County, North Carolina, in the middle of a huge redesign project involving its Human Services Department. The department's leaders surveyed the staff members to find out which forms of communications were most effectively keeping them aware of the major

FIGURE 11.1. As-Is Travel Process.

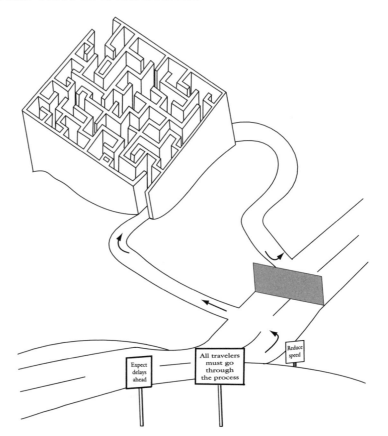

FIGURE 11.2. To-Be Travel Process.

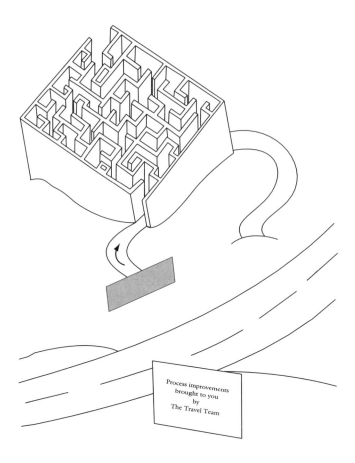

Process improvements brought to you by The Travel Team

changes occurring. The leaders asked, "Where have you gotten most of your information on Human Services Re-engineering?"

The results:

Department heads or supervisors	68 percent
Chair or member of work group or committee	38 percent
Redesign project bulletin boards	39 percent
Agency newsletter	39 percent

NOTE: Staff could identify more than one source, which is why the numbers exceed 100 percent.

This survey indicates that people are most interested in hearing about change from their supervisor. Larkin and Larkin (1996) report that four research studies conducted between 1980 and 1990 all came to the same conclusion—employees, especially frontline employees, are most likely to believe information that comes from their immediate supervisors. Senior managers have a role to play in communication efforts, but they shouldn't try to be the source of all information about a redesign project.

This suggests a two-part approach to informing employees about a major change:

1. Senior management briefs the middle managers and first-level supervisors about the change. After the briefing, the senior managers ask for feedback about the message and give middle managers and supervisors time to meet and discuss what they heard. Then, they share their feedback about how they reacted to the message, and the senior management revises it as needed. Senior managers then share the revised statement with the managers and supervisors.

2. First-level supervisors then take the message about the change to their troops. In doing so, they need to remember what we noted in Chapter Four; when confronted with a change, most people will ask the following questions:

   Why this change?
   What's in it for me (WIIFM)?

The supervisors need to be prepared to answer these and other questions. Having had time and access to senior managers early in the process, supervisors will be able to answer these questions in a credible way.

The Wake County survey also has implications about the ideal communication format. Most of the staff members said they preferred to learn about changes through direct, face-to-face communications. They wanted time, in small groups, to learn what was going on, to ask questions, and to receive direct, credible answers. This form of communicating isn't the most efficient (at least in the short run), but it is clearly very effective.

Involving People

Activities that involve people are usually the most powerful means of communication. Here are some examples:

- Summarize the information from mapping the as-is process and from interviewing stakeholders. Send that information around the organization (hard copy is OK, E-mail is far better). Ask for comments and analysis.

- Regard all design team activities as opportunities for organizational involvement and support. The design team does not have to do all the work itself! The design team and sponsor should look for ways to involve other employees when it's time to do any of the following:

Lead focus group interviews
Conduct customer surveys
Benchmark other organizations' processes
Analyze the need for new hardware and software

- Some design teams feel very possessive of their work. That's often the understandable result of being so involved and invested in it. However, they make a big mistake if no other staff members have input into the team's deliberations.

COURTING STAKEHOLDERS

Segment the stakeholders. There are many types, and they have different interests. Some are more critical to your success than others.

Here are some examples of key stakeholder groups.

- *Informal leaders:* They can block your path if they don't like your direction.

What they need: They should receive early invitations to make individual critiques of the project plan and to offer reactions and advice at each step.

- *Human resource staff:* You'll need their help when it's time to implement the plan.

What they need: They should have opportunities to give input, especially as staff roles for the new process are developed. Ask them what implications they see for any proposed changes.

- *Information technology staff:* Their help is critical in complex change efforts. The time to start visiting with them is near the beginning; don't wait until implementation. These staff members may see options for change that others don't see, because techies are aware of emerging technologies and capabilities that open up new ways of doing work.

What they need: They need to be heard and to have their input considered early.

- *Those who work in the current process:* Some of these people will be on the design team, but most won't. If they don't have an opportunity to tell you what's wrong with the current process, what frustrates them about it, and how it could be fundamentally improved, don't expect their immediate support. They won't embrace your new design eagerly because it will be just that—yours, not theirs.

What they need: They need time, attention, and the assurance that the technical requirements of the process are being attended to by those who understand it. And they need to know whether their professional identity will change with the redesign.

• *Senior managers:* In many organizations, they don't work particularly well together. They may be civil to each other and may appear to make decisions by consensus, but often there isn't a real team at the top. As Katzenbach and Smith (1993) note in their wonderful book *The Wisdom of Teams,* teams at the top are the most difficult. Although senior managers urge others to form teams, they have a hard time "walking the talk." Design team members and others may get frustrated if their senior leaders aren't collaborating well, but that's a fact of life in many organizations, and becoming frustrated won't change the reality.

What they need: They need to be assured of the aspects that will worry them. Anticipate what parts of the proposed process will cause senior managers to feel concerned; it probably will have to do with how much the change costs, whether you're coordinating with other change efforts, and whether the new process will diminish any of their control and authority. Be sensitive to their concerns. They also need to know that they're in the loop. None of us likes to look incompetent, and that's truer the higher you go in an organization. Being out of the information loop makes many senior managers feel inept. Be sure to keep them informed.

Here's one approach for communicating with senior managers. The project sponsor (and perhaps the design team leader) should meet with the steering team and other senior leaders early in the project, one leader at a time. The sponsor should listen to their concerns. They may be unclear about the redesign effort's goals and approach (even if they attended a briefing). Reiterate the project's goals and scope. And try to find out how this change effort could help one or more senior managers move forward with their own goals and agenda. Ask how the redesign project could support other organizational changes that are happening. Listen to what you hear. It will help you later.

• *Early adopters:* Everett M. Rogers (1995) uses this and the following categories to describe different people's reactions to innovation and change (see Figure 11.3). Early adopters make up about 13.5 percent of the general population. They like to be the first on their block to try something new.

What they need: They should have a chance to try the change quickly. Give them opportunities to lead pilot projects.

• *Early majority:* People in this group, about 34 percent of the general population, are willing to change and are most convinced by evidence. They are "We're from Missouri—show me!" types of folks.

What they need: They require concrete facts that the change will

FIGURE 11.3. People's Responses to Change.

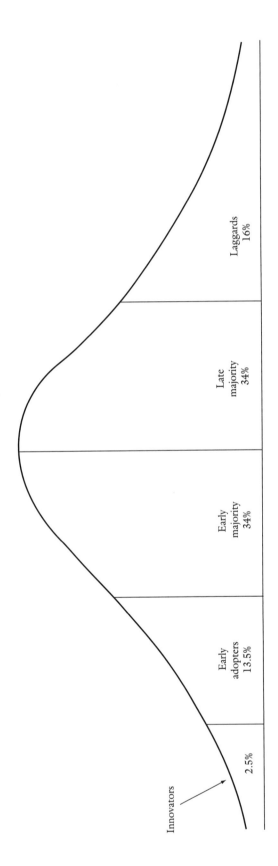

Innovators:	Create change
Early adopters:	Are first to try the change
Early majority:	Try the change after it's succeeded elsewhere
Late majority:	Try the change when convinced it's inevitable
Laggards:	May never change

Source: Rogers, 1995, p. 262. Reprinted with the permission of The Free Press, a division of Simon & Schuster, from *Diffusion of Innovations* (4th ed.) by Everett M. Rogers. Copyright © 1962, 1971, 1983 by The Free Press. Copyright © 1995 by Everett M. Rogers.

work. Give them opportunities to benchmark other organizations that have gone through a similar change. Also, invite them to help evaluate results of the first pilots.

• *Late majority:* Members of this group make up another 34 percent of the population. Like the early majority, they need evidence but of a different sort. They need to know that this change is serious, that the leadership won't change its mind, and that there is no alternative but to hop on board.

What they need: They require clear evidence that the informal leaders are supporting the change. They should also have clear evidence that those who support it are being rewarded and that anyone protecting his or her turf will face significant consequences.

• *Laggards:* For description of this group, see discussion of "opponents" and "adversaries" in Chapter Twelve.

"They Just Don't Believe Us!" Some managers and leaders have the unpleasant experience of encountering the "TEGO" effect when trying to explain the goals of a change effort. What's TEGO? The eyes glaze over! The staff members aren't openly hostile and they may not challenge you; instead, they just fade away.

What's going on? Perhaps they've heard the message before. Perhaps they want to believe but have been burned and refuse to raise their hopes again. Perhaps they see too many changes going on and can't keep them all straight. There are many possible explanations, including the fact that society is increasingly cynical, as reflected by the number of Dilbert cartoons hanging in offices everywhere.

It's All About Credibility Those who have studied communications know the two key rules: (1) know your topic and (2) know your audience. The skepticism grows more quickly if a speaker doesn't really understand the topic or doesn't show an appreciation for the audience and its concerns.

An even more fundamental communications principle is this: people tend to believe or not believe the message depending on the source's credibility.

Think about it. Why is it that someone can make a comment at a meeting but nobody will pick up on it, and then a half hour later somebody else makes the same comment and everyone nods vigorously? It's for the same reason that teenagers listen to each other but not to their parents—the credibility of the source.

Consider who has credibility with various groups within your organization and seek creative ways to enlist those credible sources in your communications effort. Different people have credibility with different groups. A highly skilled technical person will have more credibility with other techies than a middle manager who isn't technology oriented.

One last thought on credibility: those who are known for being open, candid, and honest will have credibility with virtually any group. As Will Rogers said, "Tell the truth and you don't have to have nearly as good a memory!"

Find those with credibility, seek their advice and involvement, and TEGO will be just an acronym, not a problem for you.

 **Organizational Politics Overcome the Change Effort**

 **Learn the Agendas of Those with Political Clout, and Include These People When Possible** The sponsor can play a key role by identifying the key interests and goals of those with political power, especially the interests and goals that may be affected by the redesign effort. These goals change, of course, so the sponsor would be wise to stay "in the loop" to determine when political breezes change course. For instance, the sponsor should find out what worries the current managers of the process, what they'd like to see changed, and what upsets them in their work. If the design team comes up with solutions that also make life easier for the current process managers, the team is likely to have allies when it makes its final report.

Keep two political truisms in mind when moving through your change project.

1. When political needs collide with professional desires, the political ones usually win out. If elected officials or political appointees decide that they need to do something because the politics of the situation requires it, civil servants will find it tough to win them over by saying, "But what you're contemplating violates my professional judgment!" One hopes that the professionals' views were already factored in, but at the end of the day if the professional and political needs conflict, the political views typically prevail. Thus, change agents must understand the political agendas and needs of senior officials. One strategy that works well is to show how the change project supports some element of senior officials' political agendas.

2. Harlan Cleveland, a grand old man of public administration, once said that the key for civil servants is to learn how to think politically without becoming (or being perceived as) political. Change agents are foolish to ignore political agendas. However, they risk losing their credibility with professional colleagues if they become immersed in political activities. Learn how the political people operate, respect their points of view, understand why their time frame is short, and then use this information to craft a change plan that makes sense to all key stakeholders.

SUMMARY

This chapter detailed the *how* of communications during change. It looked at a hierarchy of communications effectiveness, from listening (least effective) to involving people (most effective). It also revisited the two questions people tend to ask when a change is announced: "Why this change?" and "What's in it for me?" Change agents and communications people must be ready to provide credible answers to these questions. These tips are all related to two of our three *p*'s: the communications *plan* and the *people* involved in the change. This chapter delved further into the people dimension by pointing out the need to "segment" the audience; it discussed several groups that need to receive information and be included during the change effort.

Finally, this chapter addressed the politics of change. Unfortunately, wonderful change efforts sometimes get derailed (at least for a while) because of shifting political breezes. Most government staff aren't in a position to have a major impact on the environment that influences their political officials. However, change leaders must develop good antennae so that they can anticipate and understand the political agendas of key officials and tie some of the change project's goals to those agendas. The next, and final, chapter will discuss this need further.

CHAPTER 12

Building a Bridge from Design to Implementation

Implementation is, ultimately, what government is all about.

—Gordon Chase and Elizabeth Reveal,
How to Manage in the Public Sector

Perhaps the biggest source of organizational disappointment with change efforts has to do with implementation, or more specifically, the *lack* of implementation. Many teams come up with wonderful proposals, new designs, creative ideas . . . only to have them become shelfware that never sees the light of day. According to consultant and author Doug Smith (1996), from 66 percent to 80 percent of organizational change efforts fail to achieve their stated goals. When this happens, organizational cynicism grows and the next effort faces steeper odds.

EXAMPLE:

True Story: I assisted a large state agency in redesigning its travel process. The team leader kept the group on task, and after about nine months of hard work, the team presented its new design to the steering team. The steering team was delighted and applauded the design team's work.

When the meeting was about to break up, I suggested that everyone had a right to feel so good about the effort because the team had come up with a winner. Then I added that we'd better start thinking quickly about implementation. The silence in the room was deafening!! Nobody wanted to think about implementation then. They wanted to enjoy the warm glow of apparent success. Who could blame them? The new design was wonderful, it made the steering team look good, and the design team members felt on top of the world. So we didn't talk about implementation at the meeting. Someone was later put in charge of implementation, and I didn't continue with the project.

A year later, I called the organization to see how the implementation was coming along and was saddened to learn that nothing had been implemented. Nothing. Nada. Zippo. People were still hopeful and nobody had torpedoed the project, but crises had occurred and the person leading the implementation didn't appear to have a game plan.

How do you avoid this problem? Stated more positively, how can you ensure that the new process design is implemented? This chapter will deal with this question in two ways:

1. By emphasizing one key strategy throughout implementation—generating frequent, visible successes

2. By providing a model that deals with the three *p*'s: the *people,* the *plan,* and the *politics*

GENERATING FREQUENT, VISIBLE SUCCESSES

There are many ways to demonstrate progress during a major change, whether by reducing the number of approvals needed, providing larger jobs for staff, enabling a customer to obtain the full service in one stop, or running a pilot and showing the improvements. The key point is simple and powerful—people need ongoing evidence of success. Here's the reverse of that—you can't plan for a year or longer and expect anyone to remember, much less support, the change.

There are many reasons that it makes sense to generate frequent, visible successes, and several reasons that this strategy is often overlooked. It makes sense because it gives people hope, generates enthusiasm, helps convince those who have some doubts, makes it easier for senior officials to support the change, and creates the constituency for change that we've emphasized. Why is it overlooked? Some design teams become perfectionistic and want every last detail worked out; they may fear failure. In addition, ours is a "gotcha" culture that only accepts perfection and that prefers analysis to action.

Think of it this way. When you look at a tall stairway from a distance, it looks like one huge hurdle. As you draw closer, you see the individual steps; each one is small. That's a good metaphor for major change. It is accomplished through dozens of small steps. And the steps must be visible—your stakeholders need to see the tangible signs of progress.

IMPLEMENTING THE DESIGN: ONE MODEL

The following model is meant to be a starting point, not a rigid prescription to follow. Study it and modify it to fit your culture. Again, I'll focus on three primary areas: the people, the plan, and politics.

The People

During implementation, the steering team again takes the lead. Its efforts should be primarily focused on the people and the politics. I'll begin with the people.

The Steering Team

The senior leaders continue to play key roles as implementation moves forward. Their responsibilities include

- Forming the implementation team.

- Writing an implementation charter.

- Ensuring that a communications strategy exists and is used.

- Dealing with those who resist or oppose the new process. (Some of these dissidents may have kept a low profile during the design phase, waiting to see if the to-be process would be approved. Once it was approved, they emerged. It's critical that senior leaders deal with them directly and firmly.)

- Keeping in touch with elected officials or political appointees and the political issues that may threaten successful implementation of the to-be process.

Later in the chapter, I will explore some of these topics further.

The Implementation Team

The steering team needs to decide who will actually implement the new process. It can do this by consulting with the project sponsor and design team leader to learn which design team members should be invited to continue their work through implementation. The steering team should also ask about other employees who made significant contributions during the design phase.

Shouldn't the design team simply become the implementation team? Not necessarily. Even when the design team has worked extremely well together and wants to remain intact, there are reasons that some changes can be useful. Moderate and large projects typically take one to three years to implement fully, and team members can burn out if they stick with it for that long. Some design teams become overly possessive of their project, which can reduce input and involvement from others. The team may also become "stuck" and be less than open to new thinking.

I suggest that some members of the design team continue through implementation and that some new people be brought on as well. The project sponsor should be helpful in deciding which people to keep and which to add. Some design team members will be happy to be replaced, because they will want more time for their ongoing job. Others may be reluctant to leave. To avoid dissension, look for ways to keep past members involved during implementation (for example, by being on a communications task force or by leading a pilot effort). One person who must be on the implementation team is the process owner; having been approved to oversee the new process, that person has a huge stake in its success and should have a key role in implementation.

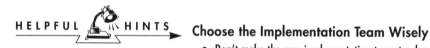 HELPFUL HINTS

Choose the Implementation Team Wisely

- Don't make the core implementation team too large. Having six to eight people usually works well, supplemented by others who take on specific tasks as needed.

- Steering team members should talk with those who supervise implementation team members to ensure the supervisors' support. Steering team members need to clarify the time demands of the project and ask that team members be relieved of certain ongoing tasks and responsibilities to give ample time to the implementation project.

- Implementation can be very time consuming. Be creative in dealing with the time issue. You might ask someone who has retired from your organization to join the implementation team. Look for someone you know. That person should have a good track record in terms of follow-through, should still be interested in the organization, and should have no particular ax to grind.

- Another approach to the time issue is to give one person the full-time job of being the implementation team leader. Small agencies usually can't do this, but organizations with several hundred or more employees often can, especially if the project is a high priority.

NOTE: Making implementation someone's full-time job doesn't means it's now a one-person task! You still need a team and plenty of supporting roles. But this approach can speed up the overall effort.

- Unlike design team members, implementation team members needn't be great at out-of-the-box thinking. It is far more important that they are persistent, able to stay focused on the task, endowed with interpersonal skills, and committed to seeing the project through to completion.

Those Who Work on the New Process

We've talked about steering team responsibilities and the composition of the implementation team. But what about those who run the process being redesigned? They'll have a host of questions and concerns about the to-be process, and they need answers.

Worksheet 12.1 contains a tool that has proven very useful for employees going through a major change. I adapted this job analysis sheet from a tool discussed in Doug Smith's fine book *Taking Charge of Change* (1996). The job analysis sheet is both simple and powerful. It lays out the key changes that an employee can expect when a new way of doing the work has been developed. I suggest that managers and their direct reports sit down together and discuss the changes that the to-be process is likely to cause. Then the manager should fill out the job analysis sheet, share it with the employee, and discuss it. Not everything can be anticipated about the new job, of course, but this form at least focuses both people on the major questions to be answered. And it will give employees a precious commodity during a major change—information. Armed with this information, the employee can proceed with whatever training, discussions with supervisors, and changes in job descriptions are needed.

The Plan

Implementing medium-sized and large projects is an exercise in energy and detailed concentration. Unlike the design phase, which is characterized by creativity, an implementation plan requires great attention to detail and to the relationships between the various phases and steps involved. Here are the major steps you should consider for your plan:

1. Develop a charter.

2. Establish a communication strategy.

3. Hold an "all-hands meeting" to review the model.

4. Prepare a detailed implementation plan.

5. Run pilot tests, revising the to-be process if needed.

6. Implement short-term changes.

7. Phase in longer-term changes.

8. Measure the performance of the new process.

I'll discuss each of these in order.

WORKSHEET 12.1. Job Analysis Sheet.

CATEGORY	PREVIOUS DESCRIPTION	NEW DESCRIPTION	ASSISTANCE NEEDED AND AVAILABLE
Role(s)	_____	_____	_____
	_____	_____	_____
Job objectives	_____	_____	_____
	_____	_____	_____
Performance measures	_____	_____	_____
	_____	_____	_____
Skills needed	_____	_____	_____
	_____	_____	_____
Knowledge needed	_____	_____	_____
	_____	_____	_____
Key relationships	_____	_____	_____
	_____	_____	_____
Work style	_____	_____	_____
	_____	_____	_____
Criteria for success	_____	_____	_____
	_____	_____	_____

1. Develop a Charter

The steering and implementation teams should jointly craft a charter for implementation that should include several key components.

• The charter should clarify how frequently the implementation team should report to the steering team and to other stakeholders. This is the key to keeping implementation on track. Don't make the mistake of saying, "This is all due in a year. Here are your people. Here are your resources. Let us know how you all are doing, and don't forget to write!" Teams need some focus and discipline at this point. Remember: implementation isn't primarily about creativity; it's about execution. Help the implementation team execute by giving it specific reporting dates. Ask the team what it expects to achieve by each date, and hold it to those milestones (or change the dates if they prove unrealistic).

• The charter should establish an expected completion date.

• The charter should clarify procedures to follow when problems arise, when milestones won't be met, and so forth.

• The charter should restate the basic philosophy or principles that underlie the new process. The charter should also show how the project fits into the organization's overall strategic plan.

• The charter should emphasize that any changes that the implementation team wishes to make in the to-be design must be consistent with the philosophy, principles, and strategy laid out in the business case. Otherwise, the steering team needs to approve such changes.

• The charter should identify the parameters within which the implementation team can work without needing the steering team's approval.

• The charter should determine what resources are available to support implementation.

 **HELPFUL HINT**

Revise the Implementation Charter Later, if Necessary When the steering team and implementation team meet during the first two to three months of implementation, they should discuss the charter again and revise it as needed. Both teams may think of changes that weren't apparent when the charter was first written.

2. Establish a Communication Strategy

Another key aspect of the implementation plan relates to communication. As was true during the design phase, someone needs to be responsible for keeping others informed, getting feedback, and helping stakeholders to feel involved.

Communication may be handled by the implementation team, one or two members of the implementation team, or a different group altogether. Again, think of communications as an opportunity to involve new people. Find people who enjoy and have a talent for graphics. And look for people who simply like talking with others and who are enthusiastic without seeming hopelessly naive. Often, secretaries and support staff members play very useful roles in a communication effort. Recruit some of them.

3. Hold an "All-Hands Meeting"

Before the implementation team starts its detailed work, the steering team should convene everyone involved in the project for a one- to two-hour meeting. Invite all key stakeholders in the project—the implementation team, the design team, the communications team, the original project sponsor, the process owner, and other key stakeholders (including external customers of the process, if possible).

Use the meeting to ensure that everyone has an opportunity to give input, that everyone hears the same thing at the same time, and that all leave with the same expectations. (Remember: one of your strategies is to manage expectations; that's best done up front.) The meeting should cover the following:

- Key principles and philosophy of the to-be process

- The charter

- The likely timetable

- The implementation team's role and parameters

- The communications team's role and the importance of its work

- Dates on which the implementation team should check in with the steering team

- The people to contact when a change in the to-be design is recommended

- The way progress will be measured

There is a symbolic as well as substantive need for this meeting. Besides clarifying and managing expectations, it reinforces the importance of maintaining communication between the various teams. It sends a clear, early signal that "We're all in this together" and that everyone has a responsibility to keep others informed and involved. It also emphasizes that the design phase is over, that this is about implementation, and that everyone is expected to support the effort, not debate it to death. If all stakeholders have been involved during the design phase, they have had ample time for analysis and input. Now it's time to get on with it.

Make the All-Hands Meeting Casual but Well-Organized

- The meeting serves as a kind of kickoff, so make it positive and upbeat. Bring food and drinks and find a comfortable space for everyone to gather.

- Create a large model of the new process and post it so that everyone can see it easily. You can use a detailed flow chart, but some people's eyes glaze over with too much detail. It's better to show the following aspects of the new process: the main changes from the old to the new, the features it offers, its expected performance, and the way it will achieve that performance level. A simple, large sign or two would do for small and medium-sized groups.

CONSIDERATIONS	AS-IS PROCESS	TO-BE PROCESS
Cycle time		
Number of steps		
Customer satisfaction (for example, low, medium, high)		
Major proposed changes		
Time needed for implementation		
Issues that need discussion		

- If you have a large number of people attending (say, forty or more), use a facilitator. For small group discussions at the meeting, provide a neutral facilitator who can use flip charts and markers. After reviewing the key points of the new process, the implementation charter, and so forth, pose some straightforward questions for each group to discuss: What do group participants like about the proposed process? What worries them? What questions do they have? What suggestions do they have for implementation?

- For each group, have one person report on and post the results and then reopen the discussion for further comments. You should collect the data and report back within a short period of time. This kind of meeting works well if you prepare carefully, listen well, and follow up on the ideas offered. You don't have to agree with all ideas, but you do have to respond to them.

- Consider repeating the all-hands meeting about six months down the road. It can help to remind people how much has been accomplished. (That's important when it takes a year or more to complete implementation.) Having another meeting also provides a mid-course correction mechanism.

4. Prepare a Detailed Implementation Plan

Now is the time to create a detailed implementation plan. Many tools and methods for scheduling work can help you determine what happens when. For very complex projects, teams should consider using

PERT and CPM methods (see Appendix F), as well as project management software. For simpler projects, teams will find the Gantt chart easy to learn and use.

Creation of a Gantt Chart

A Gantt chart is a project-scheduling tool that helps teams plan activities and timelines and that allows teams to compare their plan with their actual accomplishments. To create a Gantt chart, you need to perform the following steps.

1. Identify the major categories of work that must be done: running pilot tests, training staff, developing or purchasing new information systems or software, revising position descriptions, making policy changes, and so forth.

2. List these categories vertically along the left side of a sheet of paper.

3. Show the flow of time in weeks and months horizontally, along the top of the sheet.

4. Sequence the categories or phases of work according to the order in which they will be performed. For instance, pilot-test results need to be analyzed before anyone can define the specific tasks to be done by newly created positions or before anyone can specify the training needed.

5. Estimate the amount of elapsed time needed to complete each category or phase of work in a category. For example, decide how long it will take to conduct and analyze pilots, train staff for the pilot, write new policies, have new policies approved, and so forth.

6. Determine which categories or phases should begin first. Two criteria should guide teams on this decision:

    Which of the activities that can be completed relatively quickly would make a positive, visible difference for the customers of the process or for the staff members who perform it?

    Which activities or phases will take the longest to complete? This relates to the "critical path" of your project, which is discussed in Appendix F.

    Once you have identified the longer phases, start those early.

7. Plan the schedule, showing the expected beginning and ending dates for each category or phase of work.

8. Use the Gantt chart as a project status map. When there has been progress in a category of work, use markers or movable plastic

strips to compare the current status with the plan. Post the Gantt chart where the team meets, providing a constant reminder of whether you are on time, whether the plan needs to be changed, whether additional people or resources are needed to keep the project on track, and so forth.

Gantt Chart Example

Let's say you are given the task of preparing a facility to create a new product.* To begin using a Gantt chart, list the activities involved, as well as the anticipated time interval to complete each activity, as follows:

A. Design production tooling (3 weeks).

B. Prepare manufacturing drawings (2 weeks).

C. Prepare production facility to receive new tooling and parts (5 weeks).

D. Purchase tooling (7 weeks).

E. Purchase production parts (4 weeks).

F. Assemble parts (1 week).

G. Install tools (2 weeks).

H. Test (1 week).

Next, do some research to determine which activities must be initiated before others. You make the following decisions:

A must precede D.

C and D must be completed before F and G can start.

B must precede E.

E must precede F.

F and G must be completed before H can begin.

Now you're ready to write your Gantt chart.

---

*The production facility example is taken from UVA-OM-0294 "Network Planning: Scheduling Techniques for Project Managers," and is to be used as the basis for class discussion rather than to illustrate either effective or ineffective handling of an administrative situation, written by Ed Davis, with Gail Ann Zarwell and J. W. Ellis. © 1981, Darden Graduate Business School Foundation. Preview the Darden case abstracts at: www.darden/case/bib.

FIGURE 12.1. Sample Gantt Chart.

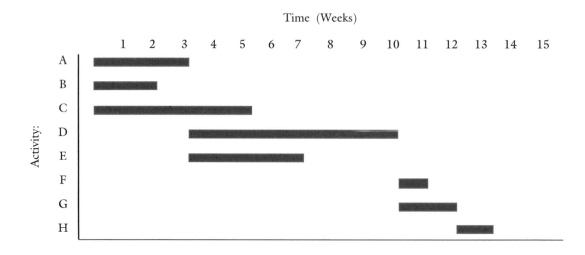

Using the Gantt Chart

Once you have completed the Gantt chart, you can use it for several purposes.

  1. Designate a lead person for each activity, note that person's name on the chart, and use the chart for regular reviews of the process.

  2. Use the chart to compare accomplishments with planned milestones. The chart offers a good visual representation of where you are and where you need to be.

  3. Use the chart as a communication and marketing tool. Once it is complete and agreed upon, it can help key stakeholders and others understand the phases of the implementation plan. The chart can be sent to employees and others every three to six months as a progress report. (Of course, this idea makes more sense if the actual progress is on target!)

NOTE: Large, complex redesign projects require more sophisticated tools than a Gantt chart. For guidance on how to use one such tool, see Appendix F.

5. Run Pilot Tests, Revising the To-Be Process if Needed

There are two important reasons to pilot test all or parts of a new process.

The first reason is to learn more about the process. It's difficult, if not impossible, to plan an entirely new process and to get it "right" on paper. Typically, things don't work quite the way we plan them. The best way to learn about the problems of a new process is to test it. A pilot test can help you learn

- The kinds of skills needed to manage the to-be process

- The related training needed

- The actual (not planned) performance potential

- Unanticipated consequences for those managing the process, for others in the organization who might be affected by the new process, and for end users

- Hidden costs that couldn't be anticipated during the design phase

- The way the proposed steps fit together, and whether some were left out

A second reason for running pilots concerns staff involvement. A pilot affords an opportunity to involve many more people in the implementation process. The communication team may be doing an excellent job of informing the workforce about the status of implementation, but there's nothing like actual involvement to help people understand how a new process works.

When planning a pilot, you should consider what you most want to learn. Depending on your answer, you may decide to do any of the following:

- Try the pilot in units of different sizes

- Try it in units with varying degrees of technology sophistication

- Try it in geographically different units

- Test different parts of the new process at different sites if the change is large and complex

Remember, pilot tests are opportunities to communicate with and involve the workforce. Look for volunteers, and seek people whose involvement will be helpful down the road.

6. Implement Short-Term Changes

As we emphasized earlier, the implementation team needs some early successes. It can't wait nine months or a year to demonstrate the potential of the to-be process. If the implementation effort is perceived as a well-guarded secret and if detailed planning goes on for months with nothing concrete to show for it, you'll lose the employees' interest and support. People need tangible signs of progress.

 **Produce Quarterly Deliverables** Set a target to produce quarterly deliverables. Plan to implement a change in the current process about every three months. The changes may be very minor, which will allow the implementation team to accomplish several short-term changes without a great deal of difficulty. Here are some examples of relatively short-term changes that usually don't require major expenditures of resources or large changes in the overall culture:

SOME SHORT-TERM CHANGES

- Remove non-value-adding steps.

- Reduce the number of approvals needed.

- Train a unit on the new process, implementing one or more aspects of the process in that unit.

- Run a pilot, measure the results, and publicize those results.

- Simplify forms.

- Change position descriptions to reflect the new tasks and roles.

- Have staff members perform the process in close connection with their end users so the staff members can shorten the feedback loop and see the results of their work.

7. Phase in Longer-Term Changes

In general, longer-term changes are improvements that

- Require funding not already in the budget

- Involve new hardware or software or changes in existing systems

- Involve significant changes in human resources areas (new classification for certain jobs, different reporting relationships, greatly expanded roles, and so forth)

- Require a change in the existing organizational culture

- Require changes in the budget and accounting systems

It will work best to implement these kinds of changes if they were anticipated during the design phase and if, at that time, appropriate subject matter experts were involved (for example, from the legal, information management, budget, or human resources department). Whether such experts were involved earlier or not, they need to be involved now.

Longer-Term Changes Take Lots of Time—People May Burn Out!
By definition, longer-term changes take time to implement. Team members will become tired, some may be pulled off the team for various reasons, and others may criticize the team for taking too long.

See the Opportunities in Team Member Turnover Don't be discouraged if some team members are pulled away for a period because their boss simply can't spare them. This should have been anticipated, but emergencies happen and you may not have the continuity you want. Rather than feeling discouraged, see such changes as opportunities to work with new people. Ask the steering team for one or two new people to fill in temporarily. An infusion of new people can bring fresh energy and different perspectives.

8. Measure the Performance of the New Process

Once the new process is up and running, someone has to measure its performance to determine whether it is an improvement on the old process. That person needs to ask the following: Is it working as planned? Are there unanticipated glitches? Do certain parts of the process need to be revised?

Before there can be any evaluation of the process, two things must be determined:

Who should measure the performance?

What should be measured?

Who Should Measure the Performance?

When it comes to choosing someone to evaluate the process, there are several possibilities:

- The process owner, working with the staff members who perform the process

- A new, ad hoc team that includes informal organizational leaders who have some skills in performance measurement

- The implementation team (or a subset of that team)

- Some members of the design team, with the original project sponsor

- One or two steering team members

- Neutral outsiders with no vested interest who have experience with tests and measurements (for example, university faculty or a consultant.)

Even if the implementation team still has the energy to jump into the new task of measuring performance, it's probably wisest to use just a few members of that team and to supplement them with others. Why? *Credibility.* Not only must the new process perform well but it must also be *perceived* as performing well. And that requires a measurement team that isn't considered to be biased.

What Should Be Measured?

This book isn't the place to detail the many aspects of performance measurement and the difficult issues it raises. That is a huge subject by itself, and many people in government and business are struggling to learn how to develop useful performance measures. If your organization already has a credible performance measurement approach in place, that should certainly be used. If such a system isn't yet in place, here are a few points to keep in mind when measuring the new process's performance.

1. Start with the desired outcomes. The process was redesigned to meet certain outcomes. What were they? How might they be measured?

2. Look at the stretch objectives. These are usually more concrete and quantitative than desired outcomes and should lend themselves to measurement (cycle time, customer satisfaction, costs and quality). How well are the stretch objectives being met?

3. Look at benefits that have been unintentionally produced. Measuring benefits involves more than asking whether the desired outcomes have been met and whether stretch objectives have been achieved. All benefits should be measured, whether intended or not.

4. Estimate the cost of implementing the new process. That can't be known, at least not in any detail, until it is fully implemented. To estimate it, translate staff time spent on implementation into dollars. Then, add real out-of-pocket expenses, training costs, and the cost of installing new systems. Estimate overhead expenses.

5. Determine any increased costs in the ongoing performance of the new process. This figure is different from the cost of implementing it, which is a one-time cost. In all likelihood, the new process was expected to cost less—or at least no more—than the old one. Whatever the initial plan, calculate the cost of performing the new process (again, translating staff time into dollars) and compare the cost of the new with that of the original process.

6. Make an overall determination about the new process. Is it performing as expected? Are the costs far exceeded by the benefits? Are there still greater efficiencies to be achieved? Are there glitches that must be fixed?

Some People Will Expect Immediate Results, and Some Will Discount Small Signs of Progress

Defuse Critics Proactively by Sending Out Messages From the start and throughout the process, you need to manage expectations. That is, take the lead, letting stakeholders know what to expect and what not to expect. For instance, send messages such as the following:

- "We've been doing this work the same way for decades, folks, and it *will* change . . . but not overnight."

- "We need your input, your suggestions, your constructive criticisms if we're missing something, and your patience. We'd rather take a little longer and get it right than rush and replace one problem with another."

- "We're going to take care of some small and medium-sized problems in the first six to nine months; the biggest problems won't be tackled until a year from now. We'd like this process to go more quickly, and you would too, no doubt. This is like a highway project—temporary inconvenience for a permanent improvement."

People May Cut the New Effort Little Slack If there have been unsuccessful past attempts at change (say, a useless formation of teams or a TQM process), people will be less forgiving of efforts using other change methods. They may be hypercritical, eagerly pointing out the first sign of "failure" (meaning, a lack of radical change).

Combat Cynicism Through Honesty Cynicism is tough for most of us to handle. It feeds on itself and spreads like an illness. The good news is that cynicism usually covers up a person's desire to believe, to hope that change may still happen. Because that hope has been dashed several times, it has turned sour (but it still exists). The trick is to rekindle some hope—without inflating expectations.

Be absolutely honest. Express your own combination of hopes and concerns. Don't belabor the concerns, but be real with people and acknowledge that you, too, have been disappointed in the past:

There's no guarantee that this effort will work better than past efforts. The only thing we can guarantee is that if we stop trying to create change here, there will be no change, period. I'm willing to contribute to this project because I'd rather try than give up. I may be disappointed again. But I'm not willing to become part of the problem by staying on the sidelines and bad-mouthing every sincere effort at change. I'd much rather push for change, support others who do the same, and take a chance on some disappointments. It's easy to give up. It's harder to push for success. Each of us has to make a choice, and I've made mine. . . .

The Politics

Major redesign for seamless service will ultimately affect power relationships in most organizations. It can reduce the number of organizational layers, and it almost always results in fewer steps, handoffs, signoffs, and approvals. A redesigned process gives some people much larger jobs, and it changes other people's jobs. These changes shift the power that people have (or perceive that they have). And when power relationships change, there is resistance. That's a guarantee. If that surprises people, they haven't been paying attention.

How can you deal with the fallout of power changes and resistance? How can you reduce the chances that elected officials will deep-six the project because it collides with political needs? There are several steps you can take as you move through implementation.

Check the Timing

Remember one of the honored rules in politics: timing is everything. As you get ready to implement the new designs, ask yourselves and others if the timing is right to move forward on all fronts.

EXAMPLE:

I learned this rule clearly and painfully while working with a federal department whose leaders wanted to make major changes in its core processes, roles, and direction. We made a good start in our change effort and involved several hundred people on various teams that identified problems and opportunities, customer expectations, and "best-in-class" practices in other organizations.

Then we tried to get the department's principal senior officials to make a decision on the biggest question facing the department: What future roles and direction would it set? Many in the department knew that this question had to be answered, and those of us on the change team pushed senior officials to deal with it. We asked the right question—but at the wrong time. At the very moment we posed this question, Congress and the White House were in a cat fight about the same large issue. This bitter battle played out for months on the front pages of the *Washington Post*. We would have been far wiser to wait and work "beneath the radar" on other issues and opportunities. Ultimately, after two years, the White House and Congress came to a general understanding. During that time, we could have waited on the big question of roles and direction and accomplished more by working on internal changes.

Ask yourself these questions: Is it wise to implement the new process now? Do some key stakeholders strongly oppose the proposal, and do they have the clout to stop you (or to make life difficult and create unnecessary hassles)? The point isn't to wait until everyone is "on board"; that won't happen until you have the new process up and running beautifully, at which point some of your major critics may turn around and proudly take credit for the wonderful new approach! The point is to see if it's reasonable to proceed now with the whole plan.

Identify and Involve as Many Informal Organizational Leaders as Possible

Who are the informal leaders? There's no formula for finding them. They don't necessarily appear at the top of an organizational chart. The best method I've discovered is to ask people at different levels, "Who are the informal leaders around here?" If someone asks what I mean by *informal leader*, I usually say, "They're the people whose support pretty much guarantees that an idea will move forward. They're the ones who can veto ideas they don't like."

When you have a list of five to ten informal leaders, ask them the same question. I usually find that the same names start coming up over and over. That's a sign that you have made a good start at identifying them.

How can you involve informal leaders? There are many opportunities. Let's look at the key elements of the implementation plan.

- Invite a few informal leaders who have lots of experience with implementing projects to critique your implementation plan. Is it realistic? Were any key steps overlooked? Where do they anticipate problems? How could such problems be avoided?

- Ask them to help design (and possibly to help conduct) pilots that will test out certain parts of the to-be process.

- Ask them which short-term changes should be done quickly, and which need more study.

- Ask them how they think communication should be handled during implementation, and if they would like to help with it.

Simply asking these questions is a positive step. What's much more powerful is to find ways of using several suggestions from your informal leaders.

Identify Those Who Oppose the New Process

In *The Empowered Manager* (1987), consultant and author Peter Block makes a useful distinction between "opponents" and "adversaries." Both opponents and adversaries disagree with us on some important issue, says Block. The difference is that we have a relatively trusting relationship with our opponents, whereas we have little trust where our adversaries are concerned. And we need different strategies to deal with each group.

Opponents

Don't treat opponents as "resisters." After all, there is such a thing as a professional difference of opinion. When others oppose your plan, treat them with respect. The key to dealing with opponents is to "smoke them out." Tell them you sincerely want to know what worries them about the project. More important, *deal with the merits of their argument.* If they make some good points with their objections, it is in your interest to factor those into your plan. You should thank these people for sharing their concerns. If you see little real merit in their comments, you should thank them, explain that you've considered the issue and that you believe it can be handled within your current plan, and state that you'll be alert to the issue if it does in fact create problems down the road.

Whatever you learn from opponents, you are in their debt when they talk with you. People who oppose a project are very similar to external customers who are critical of the organization. Unhappy customers can be your biggest asset—if they tell you why they're unhappy! We know that both happy and unhappy customers talk with other people about their experience with an organization, but unhappy customers talk with two to three times as many people as happy customers do. As with unhappy customers, our task with opponents is to seek them out, invite them to talk about their concerns, and take those concerns seriously. Use that information as a representation of what others are saying about your project.

NOTE: For more on dealing with resistance to change, see Linden, *Seamless Government,* 1994b, pp. 251–258.

Adversaries

Adversaries are harder for most of us to deal with, because of the lack of trust. We don't know why they're opposing the plan, and in some cases we don't even know who they are; some adversaries publicly support a change and spread their opposition quietly. They may resist because they simply don't want change. Or because they like their power and resent you as a threat to that power. Or because the current process is their baby, and they'll protect it to their death (and maybe to yours, as well!). What are your options with this difficult group?

• Put the onus on those who resist or oppose the change. Without becoming defensive, find ways to remind people that senior management approved the new process and that those who have problems with it need to raise their concerns with senior management. You might say something like, "Nobody's perfect, and we probably overlooked some things in our new process. Those who see problems have an obligation to point out those problems. . . ."

• Offer them a role. If you know some of your adversaries, invite them to play a part in the change effort. This part should capitalize on their opposition. For instance, ask them to help evaluate the results of a pilot (or better, to help plan the pilot), to help establish performance measures for the to-be process, or to critique the implementation plan.

The purpose here isn't to convince adversaries to change their minds; you have a low-trust relationship with them, they aren't dealing with you on the merits of the issues, and they're not about to be co-opted into agreement. Rather, the purpose is to reduce their impact on the rest of the organization. By offering them a role, you're demonstrating an open, positive leadership stance. This will improve your credibility; adversaries who don't accept your invitation will lower their credibility with the employees who are still trying to make up their mind about the change.

• Treat the change as an election campaign. Most political campaigns are won by the candidate who persuades the swing voters—the 20 percent who sometimes vote Democratic and sometimes vote Republican. Recall from Chapter Eleven that the early majority and late majority categories are the equivalent of swing voters. If those groups support the change, you'll succeed. If your adversaries are more persuasive with them than you are, the change effort may fail.

You can influence the early and late majority people most effectively through the organization's informal leaders. If several informal leaders have important roles in the change effort, they will become natural marketeers for the change. You can directly influence the early majority by showing them evidence that the change is working—again we come back to the power of frequent, visible successes. And the late majority needs evidence that the change is irreversible. They'll get that message when people managing the change are recognized and rewarded, when policies change, when reporting relationships change, and (unfortunately) when those directly opposing the change are moved to other positions so that they are no longer able to stop the train.

• Finally, recall the wonderful advice from Harlan Cleveland: think politically without becoming political. Ask yourself, "In this situation, what leverage do I have to deal with adversaries?" Political leverage can come from several sources.

1. You can create a broader constituency for change. As we discussed earlier, you can create higher expectations of the process among the end users and other stakeholders, such that nobody will find it in their self-interest to block change.

2. You can remind people of the "pain" caused by the as-is process. Keep that as-is map and its unacceptable performance solidly in people's minds.

3. You can keep the steering team informed. The steering team exists for good reasons, and dealing with resistance to change is one of the best purposes it serves.

4. You can use the power of a meeting to your advantage. When you learn that people are resisting the change project (but aren't direct in their opposition), consider calling an all-hands meeting to discuss the project. *This is especially powerful if your steering team and several powerful stakeholders are solidly behind the project.* Invite the steering team and all other key stakeholders, and directly invite those whom you believe to be quietly opposing the project. Use the meeting as an opportunity to discuss the progress to date, successes and disappointments, unexpected issues, and so forth. Then allow people to talk in small and large groups about any concerns they have. As always, be positive and respectful of differing opinions.

   Your goal here is to offer an open forum in which those with objections can raise them. The "opponents" will do so. Will the "adversaries"? Perhaps. If they do, your best option may be to invite others to respond to them. See if some informal leaders will speak on behalf of your approach. Invite members of the steering team and other stakeholders to respond. When such people publicly support the project, it can have a powerful impact on everyone.

   And if your adversaries don't come? Or if they come but don't say anything? You can use that to your advantage, as well. Once others' concerns have been raised and addressed, you can summarize the meeting by saying, "It looks like the major worries have been aired, and we've stated how we're trying to deal with those worries. I'm assuming that we're on the right track, then, as long as we can find ways of dealing with the concerns that were raised today. Unless there are other concerns that we haven't heard . . . [pause] . . . we're through for today. Thanks for coming. We appreciate your interest and support."

   Your strategy here is to reduce support for people who quietly resist. *You won't change their position, but you can lessen their impact.* If people in the organization believe you're operating openly and honorably, that you're listening to criticism and trying to use it positively, most people won't support those who try to stop the project through devious means. You will have captured the high ground, which goes a long way in the political world.

SUMMARY

This chapter dealt with the most important, and most overlooked, aspect of any change effort—implementation. It identified one key strategy, namely to promote frequent, visible successes that show people that the change is already happening. It defined the roles of the key *people* at this phase—the implementation team members. The chapter also detailed one model of an implementation *plan*. And it concluded with several tips for dealing with the *politics* of implementation: distinguish your opponents from your adversaries; deal with the merits of opponents' arguments; and, rather than trying to change adversaries' minds, seek the support of "undecided voters" by remaining open, working through informal leaders, and using your political leverage.

AFTERWORD

Courage, heart, and *persistence.* You won't find those terms in models of change. They don't appear in organizational charts or on any job descriptions I've seen. But major organizational change isn't possible without them. Those that succeed have a good dose of courage, heart, and persistence. Those that achieve little or nothing tend to be deficient in these areas. There's no formula for courage, heart, and persistence. Perhaps they're "wired in," programmed in our genetic makeup; scientists will probably be studying that in decades to come. Whatever the source, they provide the final, necessary ingredients for change.

LOOK FOR A HIGHER LEVEL OF MEANING AND PURPOSE

How do we generate more of this precious commodity? There are many ways, but I want to stress just one. It has to do with finding a higher level of meaning and purpose in work. What gives me energy and willingness to persevere when I face the inevitable frustrations and delays of major change is to view the richer, deeper meaning involved in the change.

For instance, we often talk about breaking down organizational walls that insulate one unit from another, enhancing customer satisfaction, generating teamwork, and the like. This is important work, and plenty difficult in most organizations. One way to tap courage, take heart, and maintain persistence is to reframe these organizational needs as larger societal issues.

• Breaking down walls does more than just improve efficiency and effectiveness. It allows people to connect, find common bonds and mutual interests, shed stereotypes, and discover their shared purposes.

• Enhancing customer satisfaction can do much more than create a happy consumer. It can remind us of the joy of giving, of the meaning we gain when we act as stewards (as Peter Block writes about so movingly).

• Generating teamwork is fun and exciting. Beyond that, it can provide truly transformative experiences of the kind that athletes sometimes talk about, experiences in which everyone becomes part of "the flow" and the group moves to a higher level of performance. Perhaps that feeling was best expressed by former Boston Celtics center and basketball Hall of Fame member Bill Russell:

> Every so often a Celtics game would heat up so that it became more than a physical or even mental game, and would be magical. That feeling is difficult to describe, and I certainly never talked about it when I was playing. . . .
>
> At that special level, all sorts of odd things happened. The game would be in a white heat of competition, and yet somehow I wouldn't feel competitive. . . . The game would move so quickly that every fake, cut and pass would be surprising and yet nothing could surprise me. It was almost as if we were playing in slow motion. During those spells, I could almost sense how the next play would develop. . . . My premonitions would be consistently correct, and I always felt then that I not only knew all the Celtics by heart, but also all the opposing players, and that they all knew me. There have been many times in my career when I felt moved or joyful, but these were the moments when I had chills pulsing up and down my spine. . . .
>
> On the five or ten occasions when the game ended at that special level, I literally did not care who had won. If we lost, I'd still be as free and high as a sky hawk [Russell and Branch, 1979, pp. 155–156].

I see people acting with more courage, heart, and persistence when they find and create a higher level of meaning in their work. Creating this sense of meaning and purpose will help you move past the inevitable frustrations, delays, and disappointments that come with all major change efforts. And when the project ends, your exhilaration and exhaustion will be replaced by a very deep sense of satisfaction that something of significance happened because of your efforts.

That isn't everything. It's more than many people experience in their entire careers. Be grateful that you had the courage to take a risk.

Focus Group Example

In spring 1994, the Forest Service reinvention team proposed changes to the way the Forest Service does its work. Before writing a final report, the reinvention team wanted considerable stakeholder input on the proposed changes. It received input from both surveys and focus groups. The following summarizes the process used to conduct the focus groups.

PURPOSE

The purpose of conducting focus groups was to obtain feedback from citizens who were interested in the possible future directions of the Forest Service. More specifically, the focus groups were conducted to

1. Reduce the number of models that the reinvention team was studying

2. Learn the consequences, as the stakeholders saw it, of each option

3. Explore stakeholders' reactions to learn *why* they reacted as they did to each model

METHODOLOGY

The person conducting the focus groups held interviews with the reinvention team to ensure that he fully understood the team's interests and needs. He then wrote a first draft of focus group questions and had the reinvention team critique them.

After revising the questions, he field-tested the questions on a sample of people who represented many of the stakeholders to be included in the actual focus groups. After that session, members of the reinvention team who observed the field test helped the consultant further revise the questions. Revisions were needed when it became apparent that some members of the field-test group interpreted certain questions differently from others.

DESIGN OF FOCUS GROUP SESSIONS AND QUESTIONS

Each participant was invited by phone to participate in a focus group. Those who agreed to participate received information about the reinvention team's draft report and five program models.

The sessions were scheduled to take two hours. In addition to the consultant, two Forest Service personnel were present (one from the reinvention team, one from the local Forest Service office). These two people helped by arranging meeting room logistics, introducing the participants, and answering specific technical questions raised during the session that the consultant couldn't answer.

The design of each session went as follows:

1. Introduction and welcome

2. Brief description of what a focus group is and why this focus group was taking place

3. How the reinvention team would use the information and the timetable for completing its work after the focus groups ended

4. What was needed from the participants: active participation, reactions to the report and program models, input, and suggestions

5. Ground rules for the session:

   Nobody would be quoted by name in the focus group's report

   All should participate but nobody should dominate during the session

   Each should speak as an individual, not as a representative of a group

1. I'm going to say two words, and I'd like you to free-associate, to say the first thing that comes to mind when I say these words. The words are *Forest Service*.

2. How would you have free-associated on those two words if I'd asked you this question five to ten years ago?

3. As a result of the reinvention team's work and the information collected over the past nine months, it seems clear that the Forest Service must meet a changing set of expectations in the coming decade. Here are some expectations that others have expressed for the Forest Service of the future. (The expectations were listed.) Are there other expectations that should be added to this list?

4. I'd like you to react to some ideas that might help the Forest Service achieve its future goals. For each of these ideas, please talk about what you like and don't like, about what you understand and don't understand. (Pairs of ideas were stated, each representing different expectations of the Forest Service's appropriate role in such areas as its mission, its decision making, its priorities, and so forth.)

5. Now I'm going to describe some general models that the Forest Service might adopt to meet its future challenges. Please let us know your reactions to each model. (Participants were asked to look at summaries of the five potential models, which were described in the materials that they had received.) What do you like, and what worries you, about each model?

6. One final question. What is the one thing the Forest Service must do to succeed in the future?

Thank you very much.

ANALYSIS TO THE DATA

Within a few hours of the close of each session, the consultant summarized the responses to each question. He asked one or both of the Forest Service personnel to do the same, and they compared notes. For each session, his analysis consisted of the following:

- Looking for recurring themes among the various responses

- Noting the responses that had special intensity

- Looking for responses that built on other responses

- Looking for causes and effects; the participants framed some problems as resulting from other, deeper problems

- Noting if some comments came from certain groups of people more than from others (age cohorts, for instance)

PRESENTATION OF THE DATA

The consultant then wrote the report. At the end of his summary of questions and responses, he added a section called "Major Themes and Underlying Needs." There, he added his own thoughts and interpretations to the rich mix of responses. These were not the consultant's recommendations of what the agency should do; rather, they were his analysis of the meaning and context in which the comments could be understood.

Stakeholder Gap Analysis

USES

The stakeholder gap analysis provides a systematic way to record stakeholder needs and the relative strength of those needs. With this information, you can determine the desired outcomes of the new process and measure the change from the as-is to the to-be process.

DIRECTIONS

Worksheet B.1 (on page 181) shows a gap analysis that was done at a federal agency when it redesigned its process of handling critical correspondence. Worksheet B.2 (on page 182) is a blank gap analysis form for your team to use.

1. List the stakeholders along the left side of the analysis sheet, under "Stakeholder."

2. Ask stakeholders to identify the needs that they most want the process to meet. In the second column, list those needs for each stakeholder.

3. Next, ask the stakeholders to place a value on each of their needs by dividing 100 points among the top five needs. For instance, if a stakeholder values all five equally, they would each get a 20. If one need is more important than the other four combined, the most important might get a 60 and the others would get four scores totaling 40. Write these numbers in the column labeled "Value."

4. Ask stakeholders to assess how well the organization's current process meets each of the top five needs. Using a scale of 0.1 (very low) to 1.0 (very high), they should assign a value to the performance of each need. Write those figures in the "Initial Performance" column.

5. Multiply the number listed under "Value" for each need by the number indicated in the "Initial Performance" column for the same need. Put the result in the "Initial Score" column.

Example: Say that a stakeholder's first need is "Timeliness." The stakeholder has given this value 50 points and has assessed the organization's performance on timeliness as 0.5. Then, the score for meeting that need is 50 X 0.5, or 25.

6. Now you can determine the initial "Gap." To find the gap, take the value assigned to each need and subtract the score determined for that need.

Example: In the above example, the gap is 50–25, or 25. In other words, 50 is the highest possible point total for timeliness. This is the total that the organization would receive if it met the timeliness need very well (if the stakeholder had given a score of 1.0 for timeliness). Since the organization's score for timeliness is 25, there is a gap of 25.

7. When the new process is put into place or pilot-tested, have the same stakeholders use the process and assess its performance. Write down these figures in the "New Performance" column. Then calculate the new score for each need and determine the gap, as you did earlier. Then compare the gap for each need in the new process to the gap under the old process in order to tell whether the new process better meets stakeholder needs.

WORKSHEET B.1. Sample Stakeholder Gap Analysis.

Stakeholder:	Needs	Value[a]	Initial Performance[b]	Initial Score	Initial Gap	New Performance[b]	New Score	New Gap
Original Requester	1. Complete answer	30	X 0.4	= 12	18	X 0.6	= 12	12
	2. Timeliness	30	X 0.3	= 9	21	X 0.9	= 27	3
	3. Accurate answer	30	X 0.7	= 21	9	X 0.8	= 24	6
	4. Contact person provided	10	X 1.0	= 10	–	X 1.0	= 10	–
				52	48		79	21
Executive Management	1. Complete response	15	X 0.6	= 9	6	X 0.8	= 12	3
	2. Timeliness	50	X 0.2	= 10	40	X 0.9	= 45	5
	3. Appropriateness	20	X 0.4	= 8	12	X 0.8	= 16	4
	4. Painless to executive management	10	X 0.2	= 2	8	X 0.9	= 9	1
	5. Contact person provided	5	X 1.0	= 5	–	X 1.0	= 5	–
				34	66		87	13
Lead Originator	1. Enough time	25	X 0.3	= 7.5	17.5	X 0.6	= 15	10
	2. Clear guidance	25	X 0.2	= 5	20	X 0.5	= 12.5	12.5
	3. Manageable workload	20	X 0.2	= 4	16	X 0.5	= 10	10
	4. Status information available	15	X 0.1	= 1.5	13.5	X 0.9	= 13.5	1.5
	5. Administrative support	10	X 0.7	= 7	3	X 0.9	= 9	1
	6. Professional respect	5	X 0.3	= 1.5	3.5	X 0.4	= 2	3
				26.5	73.5		62	38
Administrative Support	1. Preparation guidance	20	X 0.3	= 6	14	X 0.8	= 16	4
	2. Timeliness	20	X 0.5	= 10	10	X 0.8	= 16	4
	3. Status information available	15	X 0.2	= 3	12	X 0.9	= 13.5	1.5
	4. One simple system	15	X 0.1	= 1.5	13.5	X 0.9	= 13.5	1.5
	5. Respect	30	X 0.5	= 15	15	X 0.7	= 21	9
				35.5	64.5		80	20

Summary of Stakeholder Satisfaction Scores

	Initial	New
Original Requester	52	79
Executive Management	34	87
Lead Originator	26.5	62
Administrative Support	35.5	80

[a]The importance that the stakeholder assigns to each need (100 points divided among the various needs).

[b]The stakeholder's assessment of the organization's performance on each need, from 0.1 (very low) to 1.0 (very high).

WORKSHEET B.2. Your Stakeholder Gap Analysis.

Stakeholder:	Needs	Initial				New			
		Value[a]	Performance[b]	Score	Gap	Performance[b]	Score	Gap
_____ _____ _____	1. _____	___	X ___	= ___	___	X ___	= ___	___
	2. _____	___	X ___	= ___	___	X ___	= ___	___
	3. _____	___	X ___	= ___	___	X ___	= ___	___
	4. _____	___	X ___	= ___	___	X ___	= ___	___
	5. _____	___	X ___	= ___	___	X ___	= ___	___
_____ _____	1. _____	___	X ___	= ___	___	X ___	= ___	___
	2. _____	___	X ___	= ___	___	X ___	= ___	___
	3. _____	___	X ___	= ___	___	X ___	= ___	___
	4. _____	___	X ___	= ___	___	X ___	= ___	___
	5. _____	___	X ___	= ___	___	X ___	= ___	___
_____ _____	1. _____	___	X ___	= ___	___	X ___	= ___	___
	2. _____	___	X ___	= ___	___	X ___	= ___	___
	3. _____	___	X ___	= ___	___	X ___	= ___	___
	4. _____	___	X ___	= ___	___	X ___	= ___	___
	5. _____	___	X ___	= ___	___	X ___	= ___	___

[a]The importance that the stakeholder assigns to each need (100 points divided among the various needs).

[b]The stakeholder's assessment of the organization's performance on each need, from 0.1 (very low) to 1.0 (very high).

Benchmarking Steps

Benchmarking is the continuous process of measuring products, services and practices against the toughest competitors or those companies recognized as industry leaders.

—David T. Kearns, former CEO, XEROX, as quoted in Camp, *Benchmarking*, 1989, p. 10.

USES

Benchmarking helps employees learn what performance standards the very best organizations are setting and how they are achieving those standards. Benchmarks offer an excellent source of possible stretch objectives.

DIRECTIONS

1. Decide what to benchmark. When redesigning work processes, this will most likely be the process you are redesigning.

2. Identify performance indicators to measure.

The following list illustrates such performance indicators.

COST	QUALITY
Productivity	Customer satisfaction
Process efficiency	Effectiveness
Cost of resources	Timeliness
	Level of service

3. Document your current performance.

> Measure for cost and quality.
> Identify key cost drivers and other factors influencing performance.
> Note possible areas of improvement.

4. Identify potential benchmarking "partners"—the organizations whose processes you will study.

> Look for "best-in-class" organizations.
> Consider similar organizations (same size, same industry).
> Consider those in different industries that perform similar functions.
> Determine what the partner might gain from the interaction.

5. Select one or more partners and collect data. You can learn about your partners' performance from two sources:

SECONDARY SOURCES

National, local, and trade press

Federal and state government sources

Trade and professional publications

Other published research

PRIMARY SOURCES

Site visits

Telephone calls

Extensive interviews of customers, personnel, suppliers, and industry experts

6. Write a report.

> Describe the process to be improved and its current performance.
> Compare the process with the benchmark partner's process and performance level.
> Propose a new standard for your process and indicate how it could be improved.
> Determine when and how the process improvement effort will be measured and who will do the measuring.
> Propose an implementation plan.

Exercises for Doing Out-of-the-Box Thinking

EXERCISE 1: HOW MANY BIRDS CAN YOU NAME?

Give your team two minutes to identify all the birds they can think of. Have one member write while everyone else brainstorms. Ready? Go!! (See page 189 for the explanation of this exercise.)

EXERCISE 2: HOW MANY SQUARES DO YOU SEE?

Look at Figure D.1. How many squares do you see? Have each team member write then call out the number of squares he or she sees. (See page 190 for the explanation of this exercise.)

EXERCISE 3: IDENTIFY, ELIMINATE "KILLER PHRASES"

Creativity consultant and author Chic Thompson describes a wonderful exercise for making the workplace more "idea friendly"—eliminate killer phrases. *Killer phrases* are those comments that kill an idea, that

FIGURE D.1. How Many Squares Do You See?

sap our energy, and make us wish we'd never tried to be creative. Here are some common ones:

1. They'll never buy it.

2. We've always done it this way.

3. It's not in the budget.

4. Yes, but. . . .

5. We've tried it—it doesn't work.

6. Don't rock the boat.

7. But we're different.

8. Don't be ridiculous.

9. People resist change here.

10. Put it in writing.

11. That's not in your job description.

12. That's not in *my* job description.

13. I'll get back to you.

14. That's great in theory, but. . . .

15. If it ain't broke, don't fix it.

16. Let's form a committee to study it.

17. Be practical.

18. No!!

19. We don't have the personnel for it.

20. (Silence).

Look at this list. Have each team member identify five to ten killer phrases that he or she has heard in your organization:

1.

2.

3.

4.

5.

Discussion question: Why do we use killer phrases?

There are several ways in which team members can prevent killer phrases from ruining their creativity. Here are three of my favorites.

1. Post a killer phrase sheet in the room where you meet. Keep it simple. Just label it something like "Killer Phrases We've Uttered" and put it on the wall where all can see. Agree, as a team, that anyone who hears a killer phrase during team meetings will record it on the sheet. That's it! No need to condemn the person who uttered it, no need to make a big deal about it. Many of us say killer phrases and aren't even aware we're doing it. If the sheet is posted and if killer phrases are written as they're spoken, everyone will become more aware of them and will use them less often.

2. Develop good comebacks. Killer phrases are wired into most of us and we've heard them from our earliest years, so it may be impossible to rid your meeting site of killer phrases completely. But you can keep them from wielding too much power. One way to do that is with good comebacks.

This takes practice. First, refer to your lists of killer phrases heard around the organization. Next, try to develop a comeback, a statement that would suck the life out of that killer phrase. Here are some examples.

KILLER PHRASE	POSSIBLE COMEBACK
But we've always done it this way.	And what results have we achieved?
It's not in the budget.	Maybe it should be in the budget.
Let's not rock the boat.	If the boat's on a sandbar, somebody needs to rock it!

Now work as a team to develop comebacks to your list of killer phrases.

KILLER PHRASE	POSSIBLE COMEBACK
1.	1.
2.	2.
3.	3.
4.	4.
5.	5.

3. Buy nerf balls for each team member. Whenever someone utters a killer phrase, *gently* toss a nerf ball at the offender! It sounds violent, but it isn't at all. Rather, it's a fun, active way to make people aware of what they typically don't realize—that they are using killer phrases.

EXERCISE 4: HOW FAR DID THE BOOKWORM TRAVEL?

Each of the four volumes depicted in Figure D.2 has the same number of pages, and the width from the first to the last page of each volume is two inches thick.* Each volume has two covers, and each cover is one-sixth of an inch thick.

A microscopic bookworm was born on page one of Volume One. During his life, he ate a straight hole across the bottom of the volumes. He ate all the way to the last page of Volume Four. The bookworm ate in a straight line, without zigzagging. The volumes are in English and are right-side-up on a bookcase shelf.

Challenge: How many inches did the bookworm travel during his life? _____

(See page 190 for the explanation of this exercise.)

---

*Thompson, *What a Great Idea!* 1992, p. 5. Used with permission.

FIGURE D.2. How Many Inches Did the Bookworm Travel?

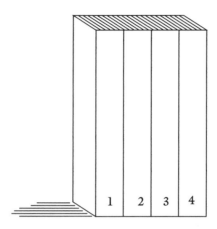

EXERCISE 5: HOW DO WE GET OUR TEAM OUT OF THE BOX?

I have learned that certain questions have a powerful impact on people's ability to think in refreshing new ways. Here are some that various teams have tried and found useful:

- Where is the law (not the regulation, not the rule, but the law) requiring us to do the work this way?

- If this were our company, if we invested our money to get it started, would we design the work this way?

- What are the costs and benefits of each control, review, or approval that we place on this process? What's the cost of caring?

- Should we be doing this work in the first place?

- Why is there any paper in this process?

- What is it currently possible to do that our end users don't know about but might want if and when they learn of it?

EXPLANATION OF EXERCISE 1: HOW MANY BIRDS CAN YOU NAME?

How many birds did your team identify? In part, that depends on how narrowly you chose to define *bird*. Look at your list. Do all the entries have feathers and wings? Or did someone suggest a jailbird? What about the Baltimore Orioles? Or Ladybird Johnson? Or Larry Bird?

If anyone suggested such names, what happened? Did you write them down? Did people chuckle but then continue without noting them? How did you, personally, react, when you heard an unconventional type of bird mentioned?

Redesigning work, like all creative endeavors, is most successful when we don't censor our thinking unnecessarily. There will be plenty of skeptics and cynics who will say that your innovative ideas for the new process aren't practical. There will be no lack of killer phrases. Your job is to think in dramatic new ways. Just as this bird exercise may have shown, we often box ourselves in. Help each other get out of those boxes!

EXPLANATION OF EXERCISE 2: HOW MANY SQUARES DO YOU SEE?

Well, how many did you see? Frequent answers are 16, 17, 21, and 24. Take another look.

There are 16 to begin with. Then the entire figure is a square, making it 17. If you look at the squares 2 X 2, you'll see a square in each corner, which makes 21. You can see a 2 X 2 square in the middle of the figure—that's 22. How about the 2 X 2 in the upper middle of the figure? And in the middle on the right? Lower middle? And middle on the left? We're up to 26.

Finally, look for 3 X 3 squares within the figure. There are 4, bringing us to 30! So, who on your team got the right answer? If nobody saw 30, who was closest to being right? The answer is, you were *all* right. Impossible? Remember the question:

How many squares do you see?

You saw as many as you saw. If the question had been, "How many squares are there?" that would be a different matter entirely. To that question, there is, in fact, a correct answer—30.

The point? When you begin with a clean sheet and start getting out of the box, it's critical to find out *what people see*. Don't think in terms of correct answers anymore; think of *perceptions*. Listen carefully when a new idea is proposed. Scratch beneath the surface of an idea to see if there's something worth pursuing.

EXPLANATION OF EXERCISE 4: HOW FAR DID THE BOOKWORM TRAVEL?

How many inches did you count? People often answer "nine inches" because they see the bookworm eating through the pages of four books (each two inches thick), plus through six covers (each one-sixth of an inch thick). Unlike Exercise 2 (the squares) in which everybody's answer is right, there is indeed a right answer here: five inches.

How's that? The backs of the books are facing you. Thus, where is page 1 of Volume One? Not on the left side of Volume One, as most people assume. It's on the right side. And the last page of Volume Four is on the left side of that volume (as its back faces us). Thus, our microscopic bookworm ate through two complete books (Volumes Two and Three) for a subtotal of four inches, and it ate through six covers (each one-sixth of an inch) for another inch.

Most people make an assumption in this exercise—an assumption that turns out to be false. We assume the books are facing us, as if we were about to pick them up and read them. And that's the point of this exercise—to help us realize how quickly, and often inaccurately, we make assumptions. Those assumptions have great power over the work we do and the way we do it. And that, of course, is one of the three key redesign principles—to surface, examine, and challenge assumptions.

Value-Added Analysis

USES

A value-added analysis can help you evaluate each step in the process. Steps that add no value should be eliminated, or they should be performed at the same time as value-adding steps. By minimizing or eliminating non-value-adding steps, you reduce cycle time, staff and customer frustration, and opportunities for error.

DIRECTIONS

Once you have mapped the current process, use Figure E.1 to determine whether each step adds value (from the end user's point of view) and whether it is necessary or discretionary (from the organization's point of view). Review each step of the as-is process. If the process has several dozen steps, it's OK to divide it into its major phases. Then, using Figure E.1, place each step (or phase) into its appropriate quadrant. This exercise gives the team a quick visual depiction of the overall process in terms of its value to end users. (Are most steps in the value-added or non-value-added side?) It also helps the team visualize how much of the process is absolutely necessary or discretionary. Once you have the process analyzed and noted in the figure, you have some choices.

FIGURE E.1. Value-Adding Assessment.

	Non-Value-Added	Value-Added
Necessary		
Discretionary		

1. A step that adds value and is necessary should be kept.

2. A step that adds value but is discretionary should be kept *if* its benefits to the end user clearly outweigh its costs.

3. A step that does not add value and is discretionary should be dropped.

4. A step that does not add value but is necessary should be assessed according to the following questions.

> Is it indeed necessary? If it is required by a regulation, who wrote that regulation? Can the organization change the regulation, eliminating the need for the non-value-adding step?

> If it is clearly necessary, can you obtain a waiver that allows you not to perform the step for a year?

> If it cannot be temporarily waived, can it be taken "off-line" and performed in parallel with the value-adding steps?

Whether or not a step adds value can only be determined by the end users of the process. If the end user cares about the step, it is value-added. Remember: Whether a step adds value or not is only determined by the end users of the process. The definition of value-added is that the end user *cares* about the particular step.

Network Planning Techniques

PERT (for Program Evaluation and Review Technique) and CPM (Critical Path Method) were developed in 1957 and 1958 by different groups. Both groups wanted to find effective methods of planning and scheduling complex projects. Designed by the U.S. Navy with the assistance of the Booz, Allen & Hamilton consulting firm, PERT was first used in developing the Polaris ballistic missile. It helped the navy save two years on that project. PERT and CPM had certain differences when first developed, but today they are used interchangeably and are referred to as *network planning techniques.* They have some similarities to Gantt charts, but they do a better job of showing the relationship between activities and of identifying the key chain of activities (or the "critical path") that must be closely managed to keep a project on time.

Here are the basic steps in constructing a network diagram:

1. Identify the key activities that must be performed.

2. Determine the relationships among these activities, including the sequencing of activities.

3. Estimate the time that each activity should take. The team could make three estimates of time requirements for each activity:

An optimistic estimate (assuming minimal problems and disruptions)

A pessimistic estimate (assuming maximum problems)

An estimate of the probable time (assuming relatively normal conditions)

4. Design the network plan, showing the activities and relationships, as well as the time intervals.

5. Determine the critical path; this path is the longest (in terms of time) from the beginning to the end of the project.

6. Look for ways to shorten that time.

7. Use the network diagram to control and manage your activities as you proceed.

Let's use the same example that was used for the Gantt chart in Chapter Twelve—preparing a production facility to create a new product.*

A. Design production tooling (3 weeks).

B. Prepare manufacturing drawings (2 weeks).

C. Prepare production facility to receive new tooling and parts (5 weeks).

D. Purchase tooling (7 weeks).

E. Purchase production parts (4 weeks).

F. Assemble parts (1 week).

G. Install tools (2 weeks).

H. Test (1 week).

---

*The production facility example is taken from UVA-OM-0294 "Network Planning: Scheduling Techniques for Project Managers," and is to be used as the basis for class discussion rather than to illustrate either effective or ineffective handling of an administrative situation, written by Ed Davis, with Gail Ann Zarwell and J. W. Ellis. © 1981, Darden Graduate Business School Foundation. Preview the Darden case abstracts at: www.darden/case/bib.

Let's make the following assumptions:

Activities A, B, and C can be done simultaneously at the beginning.

A must precede D.

D and C must be finished before F and G can begin.

B must precede E.

E must take place before F.

F and G can be done concurrently.

F and G must be completed before H can begin.

The completion of H represents the end of the project.

To construct the network diagram, place the starting activity or activities (in this case, A, B, and C) on the left side of the page. Then go to one of the activities and ask, "What should happen once this activity has been completed?" In our example, the completion of Activity A (design production tooling) leads to Activity D (purchase tooling). Thus, draw an arrow from A to D. Now ask the same question of the last activity: "What should happen once D has been completed?" In this case, two activities are triggered: F (assemble parts) and G (install tools). Begin with the other two initial activities (B and C), asking the same questions and continuing to draw arrows to subsequent activities.

The network diagram for our example appears in Figure F.1. The circled letters represent the above activities. The numbers at each

FIGURE F.1. Network Plan.

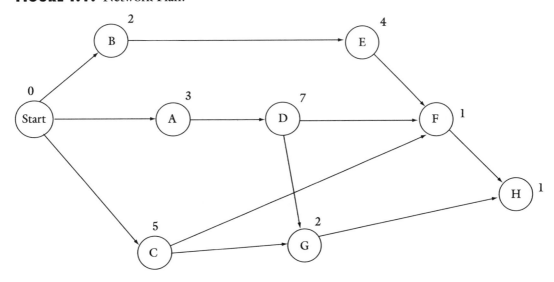

activity represent time—in this case, the number of weeks needed to complete that activity.

FINDING THE CRITICAL PATH

One of the most important uses of this diagram is to chart the critical path—the longest sequence of activities through the network (in terms of time). This concept is important because the critical path determines the project's completion time; the project cannot be finished in less time than is in the critical path. If any activity in the critical path takes more time than was estimated, and if no other activity is decreased by the same amount of time, then the project will take longer to complete.

How do you find the critical path? Follow the arrows from the start and identify all of the possible paths from beginning to end (activity H). In the above example, here are the possibilities:

BEFH

ADFH

ADGH

CFH

CGH

Next, add the cumulative time that each combination of activities will require. Here are the totals for the above combinations:

BEFH = 8 weeks (B = 2 weeks, E = 4 weeks, F = 1 week, and H = 1 week, for a total of 8 weeks)

ADFH = 12 weeks

ADGH = 13 weeks

CFH = 7 weeks

CGH = 8 weeks

What is the critical path? Remember, it's the path of activities requiring the longest period of time. In this example, the critical path involves activities ADGH and equals 13 weeks.

USING THE CRITICAL PATH TO MANAGE THE PROJECT

What can project staff members do once they have identified the critical path? They need to be especially careful in designing and carrying out activities A, D, G, and H; any delay in that sequence will necessarily prolong the project. They should constantly monitor activities along the critical path to determine whether they are within anticipated time frames. Doing so allows them to anticipate problems and to determine whether the project must be extended or not.

On the other hand, anything that can speed up the activities along the critical path will reduce overall project duration. Project staff members could shift people and resources away from less critical sequences of activities (for example, CFH, which takes only seven weeks and includes only one activity in the critical path) and could put them on the critical path.

RECOMMENDED READING

Ackoff, R. *The Art of Problem Solving*. New York: Wiley, 1978.

Appleton, D. *PROBE: Principles of Business Engineering*. Manhattan Beach, Calif.: Talon Press, 1994.

AT&T Quality Steering Committee. *Reengineering Handbook*. Indianapolis: AT&T, 1991.

Block, P. *The Empowered Manager*. San Francisco: Jossey-Bass, 1987.

Bryson, J. M., and Alston, F. K. *Creating and Implementing Your Strategic Plan: A Workbook for Public and Nonprofit Organizations*. San Francisco: Jossey-Bass, 1996.

Business Process Reengineering Assessment Guide. Washington, D.C.: General Accounting Office, 1997.

Camp, R. *Benchmarking: The Search for Industry Best Practices That Lead to Superior Performance*. Milwaukee, Wis.: ASQC Quality Press, 1989.

Caudell, S. *Reengineering for Results: Keys to Success from Government Experience*. Washington, D.C.: National Academy of Public Administration, 1994.

Chase, G., and Reveal, E. *How to Manage in the Public Sector*. Reading, Mass.: Addison-Wesley, 1983.

Davis, E., with Zarwell, G. A., and Ellis, J. W. *Network Planning: Scheduling Techniques for Project Managers*. Charlottesville, Va.: University of Virginia Darden Graduate Business School Foundation, 1981.

Friedman, M. *A Guide to Developing and Using Performance Measures in Results-Based Budgeting.* Washington D.C.: Finance Project, 1997.

Hall, G., Rosenthal, J., and Wade, J. "How to Make Reengineering Really Work." *Harvard Business Review,* Nov.–Dec. 1993, pp. 119–131.

Hammer, M., and Champy, J. *Reengineering the Corporation.* New York: HarperCollins, 1993.

Hammer, J., and Stanton, S. *The Reengineering Revolution.* New York: HarperCollins, 1995.

Hyde, A. C. "Process Reengineering: Breaking the Quality Barrier." *Public Manager,* fall 1993, pp. 60–63.

Katzenbach, J., and Smith, D. *The Wisdom of Teams.* New York: McKinsey, 1993.

Kirkpatrick, D. "Groupware Goes Boom." *Fortune,* Dec. 27, 1993, pp. 99–106.

Larkin, T. J., and Larkin, S. "Reaching and Changing Frontline Employees." *Harvard Business Review,* May–June 1996, pp. 95–104.

Linden, R. "Meeting Which Customers' Needs?" *Public Manager,* winter 1992–1993, pp. 49–52.

Linden, R. "Business Process Re-Engineering: Newest Fad, or Revolution in Government?" *Public Management,* Nov. 1993, pp. 9–12.

Linden, R. "Reengineering to Capture the Customer's Voice." *Public Manager,* summer 1994a, pp. 47–50.

Linden, R. *Seamless Government: A Practical Guide to Re-Engineering in the Public Sector.* San Francisco: Jossey-Bass, 1994b.

Martin, J. "Reengineering Government." *Governing,* Mar. 1993, pp. 26–30.

Mechling, J. "Reengineering: Part of Your Game Plan?" *Governing,* Feb. 1994, pp. 42–52.

Oshry, B. *Seeing Systems.* San Francisco: Berrett-Koehler, 1995.

Rogers, E. M. *Diffusion of Innovations.* (4th ed.) New York: Free Press, 1995.

Russell, B., and Branch, T. *Second Wind: Memories of an Opinionated Man.* New York: Random House, 1979.

Schwarz, R. *The Skilled Facilitator: Practical Wisdom for Developing Effective Groups.* San Francisco: Jossey-Bass, 1994.

Smith, D. K. *Taking Charge of Change: Ten Principles for Managing People and Performance.* Reading, Mass.: Addison-Wesley, 1996.

Thompson, C. *What a Great Idea!* New York: HarperCollins, 1992.

Tully, S. "Why to Go for Stretch Targets." *Fortune,* Nov. 14, 1994, pp. 145–158.